ANALYTICAL AUDITING

An outline of the flow chart approach to audits

Analytical Auditing

AN OUTLINE OF THE FLOW CHART
APPROACH TO AUDITS

R. M. Skinner, F.C.A.

R. J. Anderson, C.A.

Partners in Clarkson, Gordon & Co.,
Chartered Accountants

United States
PITMAN PUBLISHING CORPORATION

Canada
SIR ISAAC PITMAN (CANADA) LIMITED

SIR ISAAC PITMAN (CANADA), LTD.
Pitman House, 495 Wellington Street West, Toronto 135, Canada

THE COPP CLARK PUBLISHING COMPANY
517 Wellington Street West, Toronto 135, Canada

SIR ISAAC PITMAN AND SONS LTD.
Pitman House, 39 Parker Street, Kingsway, London, W.C.2
P.O. Box 6038, Portal Street, Nairobi, Kenya

SIR ISAAC PITMAN (AUST.) PTY. LTD.
Pitman House, Bouverie Street, Carlton, Victoria 3053, Australia

PITMAN PUBLISHING COMPANY S.A. LTD.
P.O. Box 9898, Johannesburg, S.Africa

PITMAN PUBLISHING CORPORATION
6 East 43rd Street, New York, N.Y. 10017. U.S.A.

Printed and bound in Canada by
The Hunter Rose Company, Toronto

SIR ISAAC PITMAN (CANADA) LTD.
495 Wellington Street West . . . Toronto

Preface

Auditing theory has always stressed the need for a proper study and evaluation of internal control and the desirability of selecting the required audit procedures on the basis of this evaluation. But what have been the means of achieving the desired goal? If the auditor checks all the transactions for a given test period (such as one month) when internal control is average, what specifically should he add to his program when control is poor, what specifically omit when control is excellent? Apart from general admonitions to do more when control is poor and less when control is good, auditing textbooks have given little guidance. It is the authors' belief that audit work should be consciously organized so that the linkage between control evaluation and detailed audit procedures is explicit. Each individual audit step must either confirm the systems information on which the auditor's evaluation of control was based or explore the possibility of material errors permitted by specific weaknesses discovered in the course of his evaluation. Six years ago an experimental project was undertaken to discover a practical method of achieving these ends.

The *analytical auditing* approach was the outcome of this search. Over the intervening years we have applied analytical auditing to a large variety of audit engagements, and appropriate modifications or refinements have been made in the light of this experience. This book is the result. It has grown out of the work of all members of our audit staff, and it would be impossible to list the names of all those whose suggestions have been valuable. The authors, however, would like to acknowledge their particular indebtedness to Mr. Stephens B. Lowden, C.A., who worked with the project group from the beginning and who spent many long hours developing the illustrative flow charts included with the text; to Mr. Ronald G. Gage, C.A., who did much of the preparation of the material for Chapter 9 and developed the flow charts for that chapter; to Mr. Michael E. Wright, C.A., who organized most of the work of the project group in its early years; and to Mr. John A. Craven, C.A., who

v

contributed substantially to the development work on applications to computer systems.

In recent months there has been much discussion about flow charting and flow charting techniques. If this interest presages an increasing use of flow charting as a regular audit tool throughout the accounting profession, the trend is indeed to be welcomed. The only caution which might be urged is that *significant problems arise if charting techniques designed for systems specialists are applied to the quite different purposes of auditors.* There is a real need for a flow charting approach *designed specifically for auditors.* The authors hope that both students and practitioners in the auditing field will find this book of use in helping to fill that need.

Toronto

May, 1966

R. M. S.
R. J. A.

Contents

CHAPTER 1 Introduction   1

CHAPTER 2 Objectives of the analytical audit   3
    Audit objectives
    Components of an audit
    Necessity of the current or analytical audit
    Objectives of the analytical audit
    Use by internal auditors

CHAPTER 3 Theory of analytical auditing   10
    End-result theory and method theory
    Need for standardized flow charting
    Audit investigation related to weaknesses
    Limited tests of systems suffice
    Two audit stages
    Systems audit visit
    Follow-up audit visit

CHAPTER 4 Drawing flow charts   21
    Basic design
    Selection of symbols
    Symbols used
    Some points to remember
    Genesis of a flow chart
    Recording the systems audit

CHAPTER 5 The systems audit   47
    Description of business
    Components of each section
    Flow charting and the systems audit
    Final flow charts
    Volume summary
    Evaluation of internal control
    Observations on efficiency
    Scrutiny
    Internal audit department
    Weakness follow-up sheet
    Draft weakness investigation
    Revised balance sheet program
    Proposed supplementary tests
    Draft memorandum of recommendations
    Oral reporting of points for immediate attention
    Analytical audit report
    Oral review
    Some practical advice

CHAPTER 6 The follow-up audit   78
    Statistics analysis
    Weakness investigation
    Supplementary tests
    Enquiry about systems changes
    Informal discussion of recommendations
    Oral review
    Some practical advice

CHAPTER 7 Examples of systems sections   85
    Sales-receivables-receipts
    Charting of sales-receivables-receipts
    Purchases-payables-payments
    Payrolls
    Cost section
    Books of account

CHAPTER 8 Improving charting techniques   103
    Clear layout
    Simplifying the charts
    Other problems to be avoided
    Importance of readable charts

CHAPTER 9 Application to punched card and computer systems   121
    Flow charting for punched card systems
    Computer systems
    Flow charting for computer systems
    Summarizing the EDP processing phase
    Effect of a computer system on internal control
    Analysis of controls
    Searching for programmed controls
    Proving the existence of programmed controls
    Conducting the systems audit
    Other effects of the computer

CHAPTER 10 Conclusion   148
    Conformity to generally accepted auditing standards
    When analytical auditing can be used
    Advantages of analytical auditing

APPENDICES   153
     I Articles on flow charting
    II Analytical audit report
   III Lead sheets

INDEX   161

CHAPTER

1

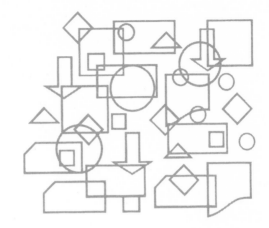

INTRODUCTION

The purpose of this book is to describe a practical, systems-oriented auditing technique based on flow chart analysis and limited procedural tests. Because of its emphasis on systems analysis this technique will be referred to as "analytical auditing." The analytical audit so described represents a means of carrying out that portion of the auditor's work which is directed at an assessment of the reliability of the accounting system and which provides a basis for planning the year-end verification of assets and liabilities. As such it constitutes not the whole program, but a very important part of the program, for the normal audit. Analytical auditing will be shown to be a useful tool for the *external auditor* on all but the smallest engagement. In addition, the techniques outlined will be found, with certain modifications, to prove equally effective in *internal audit* applications; the various modifications appropriate for internal audit use will therefore be indicated as well.

The analytical auditing approach cannot boast a long history. It is only in the past few years that it has been applied on a systematic basis over a large number of audits of varying types. However, it is a commonplace that the modern business world is a world of change. Whether welcome or not, the effects of accelerating and far-reaching change can scarcely be ignored. Business units are growing larger; automation of bookkeeping functions is increasing; accounting systems are becoming more complex; internal control features are developing ever greater sophistication. It would be surprising indeed if the audit techniques of thirty years ago were still the most efficient ones today. Auditors must restock their inventory of audit methods to suit their changed environment or else risk serious obsolescence. Greater orientation towards systems is one of the steps demanded by this new environment. And orientation towards systems leads logically to flow charting. One of the objectives here, therefore, will be to demonstrate that the flow charting technique is perfectly consistent with generally accepted auditing standards and, in fact, derives naturally from the acknowledged need for a proper study and evaluation of internal control.[1]

Finally, those who have investigated this field will be aware that many pitfalls await the first exploratory attempts. It is one thing merely to design a set of charting symbols; quite another to develop a complete audit approach fully exploiting the flow chart technique yet avoiding the many preliminary problems. It is with the thought of saving the interested practitioner these difficulties and delays that this book has been written. It is also the hope that, by setting forth the various procedures and their justification, it may hasten the day of full acceptance of analytical auditing and flow charting as routine audit techniques.

---

[1]A list of various articles which have appeared on the subject of flow charting in recent years is set out in Appendix I.

CHAPTER

2

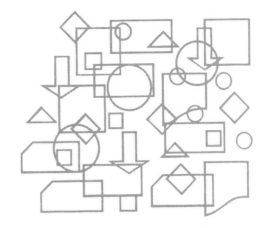

OBJECTIVES OF

THE ANALYTICAL

AUDIT

It is not the purpose of this book to discuss at length the responsibilities and functions of the independent auditor, the general definition of auditing standards, or the nature and uses of audit reports. This has been treated thoroughly in many different publications.[1] It will be assumed here that the reader is familiar with such material. Nevertheless, in order to explain analytical auditing and flow charting techniques, audit objectives must be given at least a brief consideration. Any new audit procedure, after all, must first be examined from the viewpoint of what it is intended to accomplish and why.

This may sound too axiomatic to warrant serious attention; but consider the following question. Is a given audit procedure designed to—

(1) measure the extent of a known error, or
(2) detect the existence of a suspected error, or
(3) provide confirmation that no errors have occurred, or
(4) discover what the accounting procedures are, or
(5) establish that prescribed controls are operating, or
(6) justify a recommendation for a systems change?

Each of these six distinguishable purposes could arise at some point in any audit, but each one calls for either a different audit procedure or a different way of applying a given audit procedure. Measuring known errors with tests designed for discovering unknown ones or investigating weaknesses with tests designed for assessing controls is about as efficient as using a shovel to cut wood. The audit tools should not be selected before the job to be done has been defined. The *purpose* of the audit step must be the first consideration. To dispense with this is to invite unneces-

[1]See, for example: American Institute of Certified Public Accountants, *Auditing Standards and Procedures*, 1963.

sary audit steps and wasted hours. Why draw flow charts? The answer must be sought within the auditor's objectives.

Audit Objectives

The main objective of the ordinary audit engagement of an independent auditor is:

> To determine whether or not he may report that the financial statements present fairly the financial position and results of operations of his client, following generally accepted accounting principles applied on a consistent basis.

In the majority of cases this is the most important service rendered by him. Whenever there are people who have an interest in an enterprise but who are not familiar with its day-to-day operations, it is essential that some assurance be provided that the financial statements are not misleading. The auditor's work is therefore important to the shareholders of public companies who do not participate in management; to banks, bondholders and other creditors; to prospective investors; and to income tax and other governmental authorities. The importance of this "attest function" of the auditor is, of course, one of the basic tenets of the profession.

Audits by independent auditors can also be conducted for a variety of special purposes such as assessing the extent of a suspected fraud, reporting on compliance with contractual commitments to certain third parties, or determining the price a prospective purchaser should pay for a business. These "special purpose" audits require separate treatment which depend upon the circumstances of the particular case. Most audits, however, fall into the first category—the expression of opinion on the financial statements. These are the audits which culminate in the issuance of the standard "short form" report. Their primary purpose is not the detection of minor defalcations and in the absence of suspicious circumstances they are not designed to catch defalcations unless sufficiently material to distort the fairness of the financial statement presentation. This does not mean that in these audits the auditor can be unmindful of the possibilities of fraud. If, in fact, he encounters any conditions suggestive of fraud he has a duty to investigate until his doubts are resolved. If there are no suspicious circumstances, however, and if he has done sufficient work to give reasonable assurance that no material fraud or error has occurred, then he should not continue with further, fraud-oriented audit steps merely to hunt for minor defalcations. This position has been stated many times but it is repeated here because on this point the whole concept of analytical auditing depends.

Sometimes, of course, where the basic audit is still one directed at an expression of opinion, its scope may be extended, *at the specific request of the auditor's client,* to include supplementary objectives such as examination for minor fraud, investigation of particular operating results, performance of an internal audit function, etc. In such cases additional procedures are necessary. It is still useful, however, to distinguish between the basic opinion-forming portion of the work and the extra audit steps added, so that both the auditor and his client will be aware of the cost of these "extras." Although recognizing that modifications will sometimes be appropriate where the auditor has encountered suspicious conditions or where the scope of the audit has been extended at the request of his client, the following discussion is intended for an audit directed primarily at the expression of an opinion.

Components of an Audit

An audit directed at the expression of an opinion on the financial statements consists of two components. The first is checking that the business transactions are correctly recorded day by day. The second is verifying that the balances accumulated in these records, and used in the financial statements, correctly value all those, and only those, assets and liabilities that actually exist and properly pertain to the business enterprise. The first step, in other words, looks to the daily accuracy of the accounting records; the second, to the existence and valuation of the recorded net assets at the statement date. The first phase is often called the "current audit" (sometimes referred to as "interim work" or "audit of transactions") and it usually precedes the second phase or "balance sheet audit" (sometimes referred to as "year-end procedures"). However, the timing of the two phases can vary depending on the circumstances. Some parts of the current audit may be completed after the year-end while much of the balance sheet audit (for instance, accounts receivable and inventory verification) may be performed before the year-end. For small engagements the two phases may occasionally be carried out at the same time. But regardless of the timing of the two, the complete audit can always be divided functionally into these two components: checking daily accuracy and verifying net assets.[2]

Analytical auditing is a method of performing the current audit on all but the smallest audit engagement. The terms "current audit" and "analytical audit" will therefore be used interchangeably in the pages to follow. It

---

[2]It is, of course, an oversimplification to speak of the balance sheet audit solely as verifying net assets. Balance sheet audit procedures also include review of, analysis of, and, where appropriate, more detailed verification of the various components of profit and loss.

is in this phase of the work that flow charting techniques can be applied. While the results of the current or analytical audit will obviously affect the extent of necessary balance sheet work, the subject matter of this book is the former phase; balance sheet audit procedures will be referred to only in passing. The latter are outlined at length, of course, in numerous texts.

Necessity of the Current or Analytical Audit

If the current audit is to be examined, it must first be established why this phase of the audit engagement is necessary at all. Why is the balance sheet audit not sufficient in itself? In the average engagement there are at least four reasons why the balance sheet audit by itself is not and cannot be sufficient without the current or analytical audit. These are:

(1) No matter how carefully the auditor counts the net assets on hand at any one time there can be no certainty as to what *should* have been there unless reliance is placed on the accuracy of the accounting records. For instance, if the accounting records are known to be generally reliable, then the close concurrence of a book figure and a physical inventory figure would help to confirm the accuracy of the latter whereas a wide discrepancy might call for additional audit investigation. Neither conclusion would be as tenable, of course, without the previous knowledge of the accounting reliability. Again, most tests for possible undisclosed liabilities must be drawn in part from evidence in the accounting records and depend, therefore, on the latter's reliability.

(2) As long as the net assets are to be valued on a going-concern basis it is impossible to determine the appropriate valuation without relying very substantially on the accounting records. The most common example of this is the valuation of the historical costs accumulated in year-end inventories. There is little point in the auditor checking the quantities, extensions, and additions of inventory listings if he cannot also ensure that the unit costs employed were obtained from a reliable cost system which has given accurate measurements and allocations of inventoriable costs throughout the year.

(3) When, as is often desirable to spread the workload, some assets are verified at a date other than the statement date, the reliance on the accounting accuracy becomes greater still. If the auditor verifies accounts receivable at the end of October in order to express an opinion on statements at the end of December, his opinion on the December accounts receivable figure must rest not only on his October work together with a special scrutiny of the intervening

period but also on his evaluation of the reliability of the sales-receivables-receipts system in general.

(4) Finally, the accuracy of the individual components of the profit and loss statement cannot be determined merely from the verification of net assets at the beginning and end of the year. Even if the auditor's balance sheet procedures include (as they must) a number of scrutiny, review, analysis and verification steps directed at the profit and loss components, much of his opinion on the income accounts must still be derived from an assessment of the reliability of the accounting records.

Thus, however thorough the balance sheet audit, it must, for most engagements, be based upon this first step of establishing the reliability of the accounting system. Moreover, the conclusions reached during the current or analytical audit affect the program to be selected for the balance sheet audit. If the accounting reliability is found to be high, minimum balance sheet steps will suffice to support an opinion and these can probably be scheduled at convenient dates over the course of the year. If, on the other hand, the accounting reliability is less satisfactory, then more extended balance sheet audit steps may be necessary to support an opinion and many of these may have to be performed at the year-end rather than at other dates. If, in the extreme, the accounting system is found to be quite unreliable then the entire burden of proof is thrown upon special, extended balance sheet audit steps. Should it happen that these still cannot adequately compensate for the weaknesses in control the auditor would have to deny any opinion on the financial statements.

Objectives of the Analytical Audit

The primary objective of the analytical audit, then, is support for the expression of opinion on the financial statements. This is the reason for there being an audit in the first place. The complete fulfilment of this objective is mandatory. At the same time, it is unlikely that in the performance of the necessary work to satisfy this first requirement the auditor will not encounter areas where improvements could be made in his client's systems or controls. Service to his client in this area should be a very important by-product of the analytical audit. This subsidiary purpose is, however, quite separate from the auditor's basic aim of supporting an opinion. There is no fixed requirement as to how much of this collateral service is appropriate. Certainly, there will be some situations sufficiently serious that the auditor has an absolute duty to bring them to his client's attention. Beyond this point, however, the amount of additional assistance and advice will vary from engagement to engagement depending upon the needs and desires of the individual client. In general, these collateral services are increasing in importance and, in many cases, it is the presence of these services which makes the audit an economical package from management's point of view.

The two objectives of an analytical audit conducted by an independent auditor can thus be summarized as follows:

PRIMARY OBJECTIVE (MANDATORY):

> To determine, through an analysis of the accounting system and the internal controls, the accuracy and reliability of his client's accounting records and thus to provide a basis for planning the balance sheet audit steps necessary to support an opinion on the financial statements.

SECONDARY OBJECTIVE (DISCRETIONARY):

> To give him sufficient knowledge of his client's affairs that he can offer timely suggestions for strengthening the system of internal control, for increasing the efficiency of the accounting system, and for improving the client's financial and tax planning.

Obviously, it is important that the two objectives not be confused. No amount of concentration on useful recommendations can make up for an inadequacy in the audit. Conversely, unnecessary extension of the audit will not compensate for lost opportunities to provide useful service. The following chapters will examine the fulfilment of these two objectives through the use of the flow charting approach.

Use by Internal Auditors

The foregoing objectives have been defined in terms of the independent, external auditor. Analytical auditing can also be (and has been) used to advantage by *internal auditors*. When it is, however, certain modifications of some of the techniques are appropriate. These arise out of the slightly different audit objectives of the internal auditor. With respect to the primary objective of the analytical audit stated above, the internal auditor will certainly be concerned with assessing the reliability of his organization's financial reporting in general. But his concern may not be directed as exclusively to the year-end financial statements as is that of the external auditor. With respect to the secondary objective stated above, the internal auditor will have at least as much responsibility as the external auditor. More likely his different terms of reference, and his closer continuing association with his own organization, will require him to pursue possible systems suggestions to a degree of detail beyond the scope of the external audit. Finally, the internal auditor is likely to have a third objective.[3] His terms of reference usually require him to fulfil some *policing* function to ensure that prescribed management policies and laid-down procedures are being duly followed (even in areas where these do not have a bearing on financial reporting or internal control). In this objective, again, he is likely to reach beyond the scope of the external audit. Frequently, observed deviations from prescribed procedures will prompt him to investigate situations which, while justifying some corrective action, would be immaterial with respect to the overall statement presentation on which the external auditor reports.

The differences just mentioned are more of degree than of kind. The fields of the internal and external auditors necessarily overlap but the relative emphasis they place on the component parts of their program usually differs.[4] In addition, the terms of reference of internal auditors themselves vary from one organization to another. While the following chapters outline analytical auditing procedures primarily from the viewpoint of the external auditor, modifications which may be appropriate for the internal auditor will be noted where relevant.

[3]The numbering of these objectives does not necessarily parallel their order of priority for every internal auditor.

[4]In particular, the second component of the normal external audit, namely the verification of year-end assets and liabilities, is often omitted (or very much reduced) in an internal audit program.

CHAPTER

3

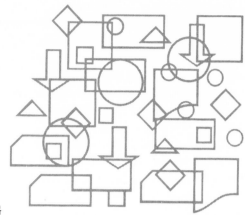

THEORY OF
ANALYTICAL AUDITING

The primary objective of the analytical audit, as stated in the previous chapter, is to assess the reliability of the accounting system. In theory, this evaluation could be approached in two different ways. One could judge an accounting system by an examination of the documents and records it has produced or by an analysis of the structure and design of the system itself. These two approaches might be described as the *end-result theory* and the *method theory* respectively.

End-Result Theory and Method Theory

The *end-result theory* would look not at the means but at the ends. For instance, one could, in the extreme, check documentary evidence for every recorded transaction for the year. Even this, however, might not be infallible since some procedural errors might not be evident from the individual documents. In any case, on all but the extremely small engagement it would be prohibitively expensive. It would mean duplicating every step performed by the entire accounting staff over twelve months—and the cost would come close to duplicating the total accounting expense for the year too. The end-result theory can be modified, however, by arguing that it is unnecessary to check *every* transaction for the year if the auditor is able to rely on the system of internal control. Under this modified end-result theory a large sample of accounting results could be examined and if they were all correct, this could be taken as an indication that the rest of the results produced by the same system were accurate. For example, if one were to examine all the 1,000 cancelled cheques for one month and find them to be legitimate and properly supported, it might be inferred from this that the other 11,000 cheques for the other eleven months were proper as well.

The *method theory*, on the other hand, would look not at the ends but at the means. Here one could attempt to explore inside the system and discover exactly how it produces its results. If the mechanics of the system were analyzed intensively and the detailed survey showed it to be designed with appropriate controls, checks and balances to forestall errors, then this too would be a good indication that the results produced by this system (such as a year's cheques) were accurate. This latter method, in other words, would go *through* the system while the former went *around* it.

Each approach, in practice, contains some elements of the other. The modified end-result approach, while concentrating on extensive tests, must include some preliminary review of internal control to justify the examination of less than 100% of the books and documents for the year. Similarly, the method approach, while concentrating on intensive analysis, must include some examination of documents to determine what the system to be evaluated is. The difference is one of emphasis. All current audits must consist of an *analysis* of internal control and a *testing* of documentary and other evidence. This much is implied in the standard wording of every audit report. The question is only one of the relative proportions between analysis and testing.

What is called the end-result approach has been the one most commonly described in auditing texts and, apparently, most commonly employed throughout the auditing profession in the past. As far as the primary objective of supporting an opinion is concerned, it is true that either approach, the end-result theory or the method theory, has a certain validity. The former makes an inference about the whole of the accounting results from a knowledge of a substantial part of them. The latter makes an inference about the whole of the accounting results from a knowledge of the detailed system which produced them. Neither inference is infallible but both can be reasonable ones, if carefully made. The method approach, however, is likely to be more assured and generally much more efficient. What the auditor is trying to do in his current audit examination is to diagnose the strengths or weaknesses of the accounting system. Thorough analysis together with a concise, well-chosen program of testing should provide a better diagnosis of the accounting reliability than restricted analysis together with indiscriminate amounts of testing. As far as the secondary objective of making useful suggestions is concerned, the method approach has a very great advantage. Armed with a more intimate knowledge of the flow of paperwork and the relationship between different procedures, the auditor is in a much better position to make realistic recommendations not only on internal control but also on systems efficiency. For these reasons the emphasis on systems analysis is bound to increase as modern auditing techniques develop. For these reasons, too, the analytical auditing technique to be described in this book is based on the *method* or *analysis* approach to auditing.

Need for Standardization Flow Charting

A systems-oriented audit plan must include some method of recording systems information accurately and comprehensively. A narrative form, which might be the first thought, proves unduly cumbersome in practice. Narrative may be suitable for some purposes—company procedure manuals or clerical job descriptions—but for the auditor's needs it is too unwieldy. As soon as any degree of detail is attempted, narrative swells to too large a size. The large quantities are difficult to absorb, related points are hard to integrate mentally, and annual changes are awkward to record. In addition, some unique problems are usually posed by the handwriting.

To these problems a standardized method of flow charting is the logical solution. First, this is the most concise way of recording the auditor's review of the system. The flow chart minimizes the amount of narrative explanation and thereby achieves a condensation of presentation not possible in any other form. It gives both a bird's-eye view of the system and an efficient documentation of the auditor's testing of it. Secondly, the flow chart is the most efficient tool for doing the actual *analyzing*. The charts clearly show what is taking place and provide an easy method of spotting weaknesses in the system or areas where improvements could be introduced. Of the different styles of charting that have been in existence for various purposes for some time, the one described here for use in analytical auditing is a horizontal charting approach. This approach has the advantage of making it easy to visualize the relationship between different parts of the integrated system. Those internal control strengths or weaknesses which arise from the way in which duties are divided among the client's personnel can thus be readily seen on the flow charts themselves, where they would be hard to extract from many pages of narrative.

A simple example may be useful at this point. Figure 1 contrasts three different ways of presenting the same piece of systems information. The first is the narrative style. While the words themselves are perfectly clear, the paragraph as a whole takes longer to absorb than a simple chart. (This difference is accentuated in practice—for the total system to be reviewed may be forty or fifty times the small simplified portion shown here.) The second part of Figure 1 shows, however, that charting in an unsystematic and disorganized fashion can be even more cumbersome than narrative. A standardized charting technique is essential if the flow

NARRATIVE DESCRIPTION

When a shipment is made the shipping department prepares a sales order form. This form is in three copies. The first copy is sent out with the goods to the customer as a packing slip. The second copy is forwarded to the billing department. The third copy is sent to the accountant. When the billing department receives the second copy of the shipping order it uses the information thereon to prepare a two-part sales invoice. The second copy of the shipping order is then filed numerically in the billing department. The first copy of the sales invoice is sent to the customer. The second copy of the sales invoice is forwarded to the accountant. The accountant receives both the third copy of the shipping order and the second copy of the sales invoice. Periodically he matches these together and files them alphabetically by customer name. Before doing so, however, he uses the second copy of the sales invoice to post the sales entry in the subsidiary accounts receivable ledger.

SYSTEM FLOW CHARTING
(NON−STANDARD METHOD)

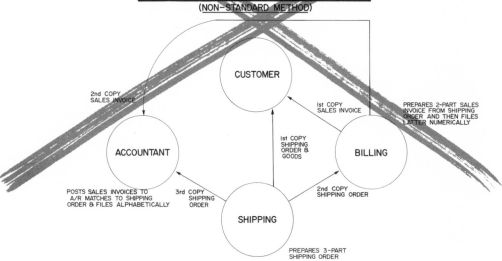

SYSTEM FLOW CHARTING
(STANDARDIZED METHOD)

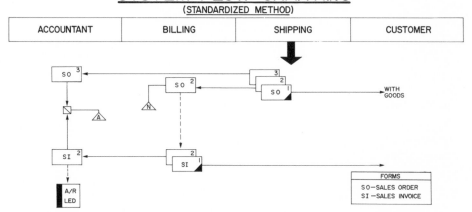

Figure 1. Three methods of describing systems.

charts are to be clear and orderly and if audit staff working together on the same engagement are to understand each other's charts. The third part of Figure 1 illustrates such a standardized charting technique. Of the three examples, it is the easiest to read quickly because it is the most organized, the least cluttered, and the least wordy. The charting technique is described in detail in Chapter 4.

Audit Investigation Related to Weaknesses

Having analyzed the system on the flow charts and evaluated the control, the auditor can then direct additional audit investigation *specifically at those areas where the internal control is found to be weak*. This ensures a direct relationship between the evaluation of internal control and the allocation of more extended audit procedures. An audit opinion is not and could not be equivalent to 100% certainty with respect to every item in the financial statements. Absolute certainty on all points is not economically feasible in the audit opinion any more than absolute precision is feasible in the accounting measurement of all items. In effect, the auditor has a fund of justified audit effort, and it is his job to use that fund most efficiently. By directing audit time towards an investigation of weaknesses in the system—and in proportion to the seriousness of those different weaknesses—this end is achieved. It makes sense, obviously, to spend more time looking for errors in areas where there is a significant danger of their occurrence than in casting about for those whose occurrence appears unlikely and remote.

Limited Tests of Systems Suffice

Before the system can be evaluated and the weaknesses investigated, however, the auditor must have some assurance that the system to be evaluated is really in force. To do this he can trace a very limited number (four or five) *of each type of transaction* throughout the system from "cradle" to "grave"—or, alternatively, from grave to cradle. This should be done at the time he completes his flow charts so that he will know he has not wasted time charting a "blueprint" system which is not in operation. This "cradle-to-grave" audit, or "walk-through" audit, or "auditing in depth," which includes both the tracing of books and documents and the discussion with all employees involved, is designed to assure the auditor that every path of the system he has drawn on his flow charts is really being followed in practice.

Why is this limited procedural test of four or five transactions enough?

The reasons are as follows:

(a) The auditor is not just testing four or five transactions in total but four or five examples *of each type* that is processed in a different manner. This assures him that *every path* on his flow charts (both for normal transactions and for special, less frequent ones) is an accurate description of his client's system.

(b) The auditor is not attempting, at this point, to prove that errors never occur but merely to establish what the system in operation is. Had he wanted to prove by his examination of sales invoices, for instance, that pricing errors were less than 1%, he would have had to examine several hundred. Fifty or one hundred would not be enough to establish a reasonable confidence concerning a 1% frequency. Therefore, there would be little point in his testing thirty, fifty or even one hundred invoices; such samples would be generally too little to establish the frequency of occasional errors, yet too much merely to establish the nature of the system in force. Since, *at this point*, he is only attempting to establish the latter, a minimum test is all that is required. A test of one transaction might, or course, happen to be an unusual case. Even the results of a pair of transactions might, by chance, be misconstrued. But if four or five, selected randomly, are examined and all correspond to the system as described to him, then this constitutes reasonable *prima facie* evidence of the system in operation.

(c) Because the auditor is examining every path of the system in detail, the cradle-to-grave audit tests over related parts of the system have a reinforcing effect. This reinforcing effect of related parts compensates for the fact that the extent of the test over any individual part is quite limited. If the auditor were only examining a few of the paths in the system this conclusion would not be justified and he might have to do more extensive tests. The comprehensiveness of the systems audit, in other words, can provide assurance, even with a limited test, that the system is operating as described.

(d) The auditor's investigation for occasional errors is conducted *after* the system has been evaluated. This allows him to concentrate his audit time on the riskier areas and minimize his time on the relatively strong areas. To perform extended procedural tests for occasional errors *before* the system is evaluated is to audit blindly. A *directed investigation* based on systems evaluation should be more effective and more efficient.

(e) Finally, in addition to his audit investigation of apparent weaknesses the auditor also performs a few extensive supplementary tests on a cyclical basis (which will be discussed later) in areas where he has concluded that control is satisfactory. These supplementary tests provide additional confirmation that the system initially tested by his cradle-to-grave audit is reliable.[1]

Two Audit Stages

For the above reasons, analytical audits can logically be divided into two stages. The first stage is aimed at systems evaluation; the second, at weakness investigation. The two stages can (although this is not essential) be performed at different times during the year—thus permitting a greater flexibility of scheduling. The first stage (or "systems audit") can be performed early in the year. The auditor's flow charts are completed, or updated, the limited systems audit performed, and the system evaluated. The second stage (or "follow-up audit") can then be performed later when most of the year's results are available for review. The weakness investigation is carried out and conclusions drawn, preliminary ideas for suggested improvements are rechecked, and a memorandum of recommendations is issued to the client. This structure of the analytical audit is illustrated in Figure 2 in simple form.

The division of the audit conveniently allows for file review between the two stages, when more senior judgment can be brought to bear on the proposed weakness investigation before it is carried out. The timing of the two stages also avoids the problem of having a detailed audit directed at the same one or two months of the client's records year after year. The relationship of the different components in an analytical audit is illustrated in more detail in Figure 3. The next few paragraphs review the philosophy underlying these various components. More detailed explanations of all the procedures are given in Chapters 4, 5 and 6.

Systems Audit Visit

As Figure 3 indicates, the systems audit visit begins with a review of the system, testing of it with a small sample from cradle to grave, description of the system and the test on flow charts, and an analysis of the flow charts to determine apparent weaknesses or inefficiencies.

[1]The internal auditor may wish to go beyond the restricted extent of systems audit tests suggested inasmuch as he is concerned with detecting errors of a smaller size. Often, however, it will be useful for him to follow the restricted basis initially to assess the accuracy of the financial reporting in all material respects. Then, as a later stage, he can plan extended systems tests to guard against smaller errors to whatever degree is considered desirable. This is just another way of saying that the internal auditor may want to extend the "supplementary tests" beyond the scope suggested for external audit purposes.

PROFILE OF
THE ANALYTICAL AUDIT

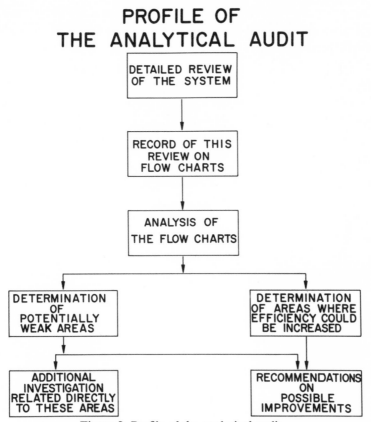

Figure 2. Profile of the analytical audit.

During the evaluation of control some areas are likely to be observed where efficiency could be improved. These observations are a free by-product of the charting already required for assessing the system of internal control (primary objective). They can lead to useful suggestions on efficiency, which should be an integral part of the regular audit service. They cannot, of course, be expected to yield the results of a major systems survey—although they provide an excellent base for such a survey should it be requested by the auditor's client as an extra assignment outside the basic audit.

The evaluation of internal control, however, is where the main emphasis must be placed. This is because the auditor's primary objective is to support his opinion on the financial statements and this depends on the internal control. While the evaluation can largely be done by an analysis of the flow charts themselves, a set of reminder questions is useful to ensure that no point is overlooked. These same questions can serve as a guide in preparing the flow charts, since they raise the points which the charts must resolve. The reminder questions are considered in more detail in later chapters.

The control evaluation will distinguish areas with satisfactory internal control from those with apparent weaknesses. These latter areas can be further subdivided. Most apparent weaknesses will give rise to suggestions for improvement to the client (secondary objective). From an audit point of view (primary objective) the auditor must, however, distinguish between weaknesses which could not permit material errors and those which could. For the latter, some additional audit work is necessary. Additional audit work required for a significant weakness may consist of either (or both) a revision in the timing and extent of certain balance sheet audit steps or a special weakness investigation to be performed during the analytical audit. Such a weakness investigation would be designed, of course, with a view to determining not whether any errors are occurring at all but whether any *material* amount of error has occurred because of the weakness.

The planning of the weakness investigation and the drafting of the memorandum of recommendations to the client completes the systems audit visit. These plans and drafts can then be approved (or amended) when the analytical audit file is reviewed between stages. The systems audit procedures are described in detail in Chapter 5.

Follow-up Audit Visit

The approved weakness investigation is carried out during the second stage of the analytical audit. The results of this investigation, in turn, affect the next step. If they reveal that the accounts are reliable, minimum balance sheet audit steps can be planned.[2] If they reveal that the accounts are unreliable (to the extent that no revised balance sheet audit steps can help) then an opinion would have to be denied. If, finally, they reveal that the accounts are partially reliable, then some revised balance sheet audit steps must be planned to compensate for the remaining weakness.

While the main emphasis is on investigation of the apparent weaknesses, the follow-up audit should also include a *few* supplementary tests in those areas where control is believed satisfactory. These can be selected on a cyclical basis so that over a period of three or four years all key areas of the system are covered. The purpose of these "supplementary" tests is to

---

[2]This point will usually be less relevant for internal auditors since, as has already been mentioned, some internal audit programs may include no, or only a few, balance sheet audit steps in any case.

PROFILE OF
THE ANALYTICAL AUDIT

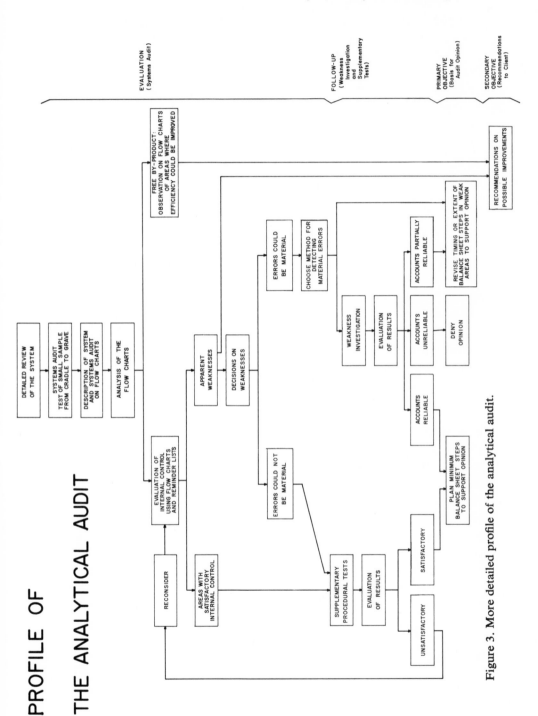

Figure 3. More detailed profile of the analytical audit.

confirm, by reference to objective data, the auditor's evaluation of internal control. It is unnecessary for him to confirm each point each year or to spend extensive time on this supplementary program, for his evaluation (using the flow charts and reminder lists) should be reasonably reliable. Nevertheless, all evaluations are subjective and human judgment is fallible. It would be imprudent for the auditor to continue year after year theorizing that some particular element in the system of internal control was adequate to prevent errors if he never tested this conclusion by checking to see whether, in fact, any errors did occur. The value of these supplementary tests is that they provide an automatic "feed-back" of objective results to confirm or correct the auditor's subjective evaluation of the system. Naturally, if a number of errors were discovered in an area he had concluded would prevent errors, he would have to go back and reconsider his initial evaluation of internal control. If significant, this could, in turn, necessitate some weakness investigation.

Finally, the follow-up audit visit should end with the making of plans for the balance sheet audit program (primary objective—for external auditors) and the issuing of a memorandum of recommendations to the client (secondary objective). The follow-up audit procedures are described in detail in Chapter 6.

CHAPTER

DRAWING FLOW

CHARTS

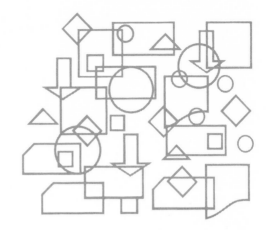

It was seen in Chapter 3 that the preparation of flow charts was one of the very first steps in the analytical audit. In the present chapter these flow charting techniques are described. Drawing flow charts is not difficult. Any standardized technique, of course, is bound to involve a number of charting symbols and conventions—but these do not take long to learn. Producing the optimum chart layout for the greatest readability is the main problem for the beginner, but this ability too can be quickly acquired with experience.

Basic Design

The flow charting technique employed in analytical auditing is a form of "horizontal charting." The movement of documents and accounting information between different employees and departments is charted as a horizontal flow between different vertical columns. The advantage of this method for the auditor's purposes is that it shows the division of duties clearly and therefore helps him to evaluate internal control.

It is helpful to have a special charting paper for preparing the final flow charts. This paper should be divided into about six vertical columns; a light squared background is convenient. (Typical overall dimensions would be about 14" x 17".) The vertical columns are used to represent departments, sections within a department, or individual employees, as appropriate. Judgment must be employed in choosing the level of subdivision which one column should represent. For instance, in a small company the billing clerk might be represented by a separate column. In a larger company the whole billing department might be represented by one column. In a still larger company there might be distinct sections within the billing department which should each be allotted separate columns.

The criterion is the significance of the division of duties from a control point of view. If the separation of two given sets of procedures is important they should be assigned two different columns.

If the flow charts are to be prepared in an orderly manner the total system of any organization must first be divided into logical sections. A convenient division is as follows:

Systems section	*Section reference used in this book*
Sales-receivables-receipts	B
Purchases-payables-payments	C
Payrolls	D
Cost records	E
Books of account and monthly statements	F

Most organizations sell some sort of goods or services (section B), purchase other goods, materials, supplies, or services (section C), pay their own employees (section D), keep some sort of record of their costs (section E), and summarize the results of all these activities in their books of account and monthly statements (section F). Obviously, there will be some organizations where a slightly different division is appropriate but for the vast majority the above scheme is serviceable. For convenience, the same reference letters as noted above will be used throughout the rest of this book (section A being reserved for a description of the client's business). The peculiarities of each of these sections are discussed in Chapter 7.

However, even when this division into sections is made, a given section may not necessarily fit on one chart. The six columns (or whatever number is provided on the paper) may not be enough to cover all the departments or employees involved. Extending the length of the chart, however, is unwise. A chart stretching out to twenty-five columns over several yards may be complete but it is far too much to be absorbed on one page by the average reader. Rather, the particular systems section should be split into two or more readily understandable components, each of which can fit the normal chart page. Some thought must be given in these cases to selecting the most convenient cleavage point. One section requiring eight columns may perhaps be most conveniently split four and four; another, perhaps six and two; etc. The columns should be headed by the name of the department, division, section, or function involved. It is desirable to include the names of the principal employees involved as well. A strip along the bottom of the page is reserved for the systems audit, to be described later. A "legend" should also be laid out, in whatever location is convenient, for explaining the form abbreviations used in the chart.

The main body of the chart is then used to outline the receipt or preparation, flow, processing, and disposition of all documents, books and other accounting records involved in the system. The main work involved in flow charting a given system *for the first time* is that of discovering the optimum layout so that not too many lines cross each other or crowd together in one corner. In working out the basic layout it is therefore advisable to jot down the main flow in rough on scrap paper first. The final flow chart can then be drawn in a more intelligible fashion. The final flow charts should be in pencil to permit revisions in future years when the charts are up-dated. Use of a plastic template can be an aid in drawing the symbols on the final charts. A template is included in the pocket at the back of this book.

Selection of Symbols

Horizontal charting has been used by systems men for many years. A certain number of the symbols are virtually universal among them—e.g. a rectangle representing a document or a solid arrow indicating physical movement of the document. As might be expected, however, other symbols are subject to considerable variation. Some charters use a triangle standing on its base to represent a file of documents; others stand the triangle on its apex. Some indicate document destruction by an "X" (as in the royal family trees of countless history books); others show it by a solid square. There is obviously no one "right" way. The symbols selected for analytical audit charting below attempt to follow the most common conventions where practicable.

Certain of the symbols, however, were modified, or new ones developed, where this seemed expedient for auditing purposes. For instance, the symbols for a book or ledger (which are distinguished from those for documents), the symbols for a general ledger posting source (which are distinguished from those for other books), the symbols for signing and initialling (which have been singled out for special emphasis), and the symbols for the check or absence of check on numerical continuity were all created because they represent different types of audit evidence or have a particular bearing on internal control. These symbols, therefore, have a relevance for the auditor preparing a flow chart which they might not have for a systems specialist.

Conversely, there are some symbols common among systems men which are less appropriate for auditors. For instance, some charting systems employed by analysts show a circle as a symbol for every "operation" performed—whether it be adding, approving, reconciling, agreeing, checking or posting (all of which in the analytical auditing system are indicated by a word or two under the relevant document). The "operation" analysis produces a more expanded type of chart with circles appearing every few inches and revealing considerably greater detail. Such a chart is useful for formulating detailed procedures or for measuring the volume of clerical work—but this detail is rather more than the auditor needs. The auditor's charts must be designed primarily to assess internal control. Charting the mechanics of how a clerk searches a file, locates a desired card, compares it to a document being processed, and re-inserts the card in the file complicates a chart whose main purpose is to analyze control. It is enough for the auditor if the chart shows merely that the clerk checks the document in question against a master card file. In other words, the nature of the charting symbols and conventions employed is bound to vary with the purpose for which the chart was prepared. Auditors' flow charts serve a different purpose from systems analysts' charts and so their charting techniques can be expected to be slightly different too.

The foregoing outlines the considerations upon which the selection of symbols for analytical auditing was based. These symbols have proved effective in audit practice over several years. Each practitioner is likely to have his own personal preferences. He may, however, find the suggestions below a useful starting point in designing his own techniques.

Symbols Used

A document is represented by a simple rectangle.

Capital letters inside the rectangle indicate the document involved (e.g. purchase order) and numbers in the upper right hand corners indicate first and second copies, etc. The capital letter abbreviations should be explained in a legend in one corner of the flow chart.

Physical movement of documents is shown by a solid line. When a document moves from one column to another column where it is used for another purpose, it is drawn again under the second column and connected by a solid line with arrow.

When an arrow points to another chart reference (e.g. "see B3") it means that the flow of this document will be continued on that chart.

When, on the other hand, the document is never going to re-enter the charted system the solid line ends in a dead-end symbol. This can mean either that the document is sent to an outsider or that it is sent to some internal department where the details of its use and ultimate disposition are not of direct concern to the auditor. What is not of direct concern (that is, from a control evaluation point of view) is a matter of judgment. The time study department, for instance, might have little bearing on internal control in one organization but a considerable amount in another.

A triangle represents a permanent file of documents. The filing order is indicated by an inscribed letter:

        A for "alphabetically"
        N for "numerically"
        D for "by date".

This shows a document being filed alphabetically.

When the serial continuity of a numerical file is checked periodically this should be indicated by a check mark directly below the file symbol. Where the checking of continuity is unimportant and not done, no check mark should be made. Where the checking of continuity would be important but it is, in fact, not done, this situation can be emphasized by an "X" directly below the file symbol.

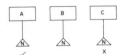

The continuity of the numerical file of document A is checked regularly as part of the system. Document B is not checked for continuity but this may not be important (e.g. the control point may come later in the system). The numerical file of document C should be checked regularly (or the auditor would normally have expected it to be checked) but, in fact, it is never checked.

◇ A diamond represents a temporary file of documents. The filing order is again represented by an
inscribed letter (A, N, or D) and the checking of
serial continuity as above. A temporary file is merely
a file of documents awaiting further processing after
some other event occurs such as arrival of the goods,
or receipt of a supplier's invoice, or the end of the
month, etc.

This shows a document being placed in a temporary
file to await credit approval and then being sent to
a permanent file. Alternatively, of course, a document might come out of a temporary file and move
through a further series of processing steps before
ending in a permanent file.

WHEN
CREDIT
APPROVED

A solid square indicates a document being destroyed. All documents must end either:
  (i) in a permanent file,
  (ii) at a dead-end symbol (leaving the system),
  (iii) arrowed to another flow chart, or
  (iv) destroyed.
Otherwise the chart is incomplete and some document has been left hanging in mid-air.

PRENUMBERED

The darkened bottom right-hand corner indicates a
document being prepared. It is thus possible to see
at a glance where the different documents on the
flow chart originate. Whenever a document is prepared it should be indicated whether it is prenumbered, numbered consecutively as issued, or not
numbered. This usually has a bearing on control.

- - - - - - → The dotted line is used to indicate that a record or
document is being used for some purpose, such as
initiating preparation of another document, posting
to a subsidiary ledger, etc., without an actual
physical flow of the first document. In a sense, this
represents "activity flow" as opposed to "paper
flow."

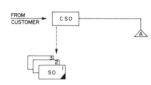

For instance, here the receipt of a customer sales order causes an internal shop order to be prepared. The customer sales order is then filed alphabetically. By following along a series of solid lines and dotted lines the complete systems flow can be traced in logical order.

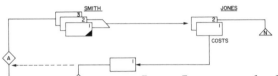

Here, Smith prepares a three-part set and files copy 3 in a temporary file. Copies 1 and 2 are sent to Jones. Jones costs the documents, files copy 2 numerically and returns copy 1 to Smith. When Smith receives copy 1 he pulls copy 3 out of the temporary file and destroys it. He then files copy 1 alphabetically.

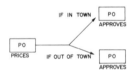

A fork in a solid line or in a dotted line indicates a number of alternative paths depending on which type of item the particular document involves.

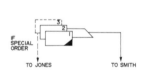

Another type of alternative can be shown by a dotted-line document called an "if copy." In this case copies 1 and 2 are always prepared and are always sent to Smith. If the item is a special order, however, a third copy is also prepared, which is sent to Jones.

A square with a diagonal represents an attaching operation.

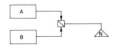

This shows document A being attached to document B and the two being filed together numerically.

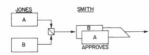
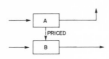

This shows document A being attached to document B by Jones and forwarded to Smith who approves both and sends them together to some further step.

An attaching symbol should not be used where two documents are merely brought together for one instant so that selected information on one can be transcribed onto the other. Here the dotted arrow suffices—as outlined previously.

Besides documents, an accounting system is evidenced by various books, ledgers and other records. Any of these which the auditor should be encountering in his audit are entered on the flow chart but differentiated from documents by shading at the left-hand edge. This symbol might represent an accounts receivable ledger, a price catalogue, an inventory record, etc. The name of the record would be indicated by abbreviations but not by initials, the latter being reserved for documents (which usually appear several times on the same chart).

However, certain of these books will be posting sources to the general ledger. Such a book is represented by a circle. The systems flow charts record the flow of documents up to the point of these posting sources. Hence, the circles represent the end-points on the flow charts. Wherever a posting source is drawn, the basic entry it records should be indicated briefly below it. In a later section of the working papers (section F) these posting sources and their transcription into the general ledger can be traced.

While the document flow frequently starts in the upper left-hand corner of the chart it occasionally must begin elsewhere. To make it clear at first glance where the trail begins, a shaded arrow pointing down from the top line of the chart is used.

Often there will be more than one start in a flow
chart. For instance, a purchase order might initiate
one chain reaction of procedures which eventually
comes to a temporary standstill until another chain
reaction is started by the receipt of the supplier's
invoice. The start of this second chain reaction is
indicated by a shaded arrow numbered 2. Sometimes it is necessary to indicate on the chart when
the reader should stop and "go to 2," but usually
this should be avoided. The chart is easier to read
if all shaded arrows start from the top line.

A small square with an "i" indicates the initialling
of a document. A similar square with an "s"
indicates signing. This makes it possible at a glance
to see where a document received its various initials
and approvals from whom and for what. These boxes
are not accumulated as the document flows through
the system. That is, the box does not indicate an
initial already on the document, but only the putting
on of an initial at that particular point.

It is often useful, however, to summarize the various
approvals which should be on a document before
its processing is completed. For instance, here Smith
gives executive approval to a document and, in so
doing, checks that it contains three prior initials
signifying that receipt, pricing and extensions have
been checked (which would have been shown
earlier on the flow chart).

Narrative should be kept to a minimum on the
charts. Small amounts can be shown on the face of
the chart. There is room for more, if necessary, at
the bottom of the columns. In these cases it is
desirable to key it to the relevant point on the chart
by means of an asterisk. Where it is necessary to
have trailer pages with narrative on them, these
should again be keyed to the flow chart.

A summary of all the foregoing figures is included in Figure 6 at the end
of this chapter.

Some Points to Remember

The most desirable flow chart is one which follows a transaction from its initiation to its ultimate disposition. Where space does not permit this, summary flow charts supported by more detailed charts are often desirable. Similarly, where a system branches in several directions, it may sometimes be best to limit the flow chart to the most frequently used or most significant paths. The least significant paths may then be covered by footnote or following narrative. The best way of showing alternatives for or exceptions to a given case must be chosen with care. The possibilities are: (1) by forked arrows or "if copies" on the chart, (2) by separate flow charts for each alternative, (3) by footnotes on the chart explaining the less important paths, or (4) by a separate narrative note on the less important paths. The choice among these four depends on the particular circumstances. Some exceptions, of course, may be of so little significance that they are not worth describing at all.

Where the client's terminology for a particular record or document file differs from normal accounting terminology it is useful to record the client's terminology on the flow chart. This assists the auditor reviewing the system in future years. Where, however, the terminology is obvious it should be omitted. A cardinal rule of charting is to avoid explaining in words what is already adequately described by the flow chart.

The flow should be kept as simple and direct as possible. Circuitous paths which lead the reader through a maze of lines and arrows are not conducive to intelligent analysis. Some advance thought on how the chart can best be laid out will usually avoid crossing lines. Employees or departments should be placed in adjacent columns if they exchange numerous documents. This avoids having long arrows from one side of the chart to the other cross numerous unaffected columns in between. The beginning and end of the chart should be clearly indicated and the flow between them logically ordered. All documents flowing onto or off the flow chart must be accounted for on related flow charts (unless the documents concerned are coming from or going to outsiders such as customers, suppliers, etc.).

While the general rule is to redraw a document symbol wherever it is being processed in some way:

some discretion must be used where redrawing would fill up excessive charting space. For instance, where a seven-part form is being circulated it may be desirable to omit the redrawing of the whole set at every position:

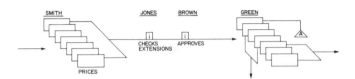

This is permissible as long as the documents are drawn in often enough that the reader can never be in any doubt as to the documents involved in the intermediate positions where they are not redrawn.

The starting arrows should be used to indicate the starting points of different chains of procedures on the flow chart, but not to indicate each type of transaction starting from the same point. For instance, if the order clerk receives three different types of sales orders at the beginning of the flow this starting point should be shown by one starting arrow, not three:

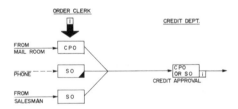

Genesis of a Flow Chart

At this point, it may be helpful to see how the symbols and charting procedures described on the preceding pages can be used together to produce a typical flow chart. This will be done with reference to the sales system of a hypothetical company, Widget Manufacturing Limited. Since in practice this systems information would be obtained by talking with each successive employee in order, the following example will be built up in stages.[1]

[1]For the sake of convenience the various stages in this example have been prearranged to fit together to form one complete flow chart at the conclusion. This is not meant to imply, of course, that each small piece of systems information could in practice be charted in final form as it was obtained. In an actual audit, only after the systems review has been completed can the optimum layout for the final chart be determined.

First Order Clerk

The chart below shows the information obtained from one of the order clerks, J. Jones. He receives customers' purchase orders by mail (together with some telephone orders as well) and prepares a four-part internal sales order form. The company salesmen also send him orders which they have prepared on these forms. After the internal order is prepared, any customer's orders are filed in the customer's file. The sales order is assigned a consecutive number from the order register and the date and customer's name are entered in the order register beside that number. The sales order set is sent to the shipper, who returns the fourth copy to the other order clerk, M. Wright, after shipment.

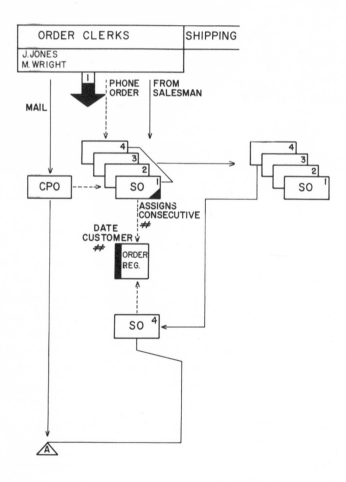

Second Order Clerk

This diagram extends the previous charting to include the information obtained from the second order clerk, M. Wright. He enters the shipping date beside the original entry in the order register. He then files the order form in the customer's file. However, if the order was only partially filled he holds it instead in a separate file by part number. Periodically he checks this file of back-ordered items and, when the stock is available, initiates a new order for the balance and files the old order in the customer's file.

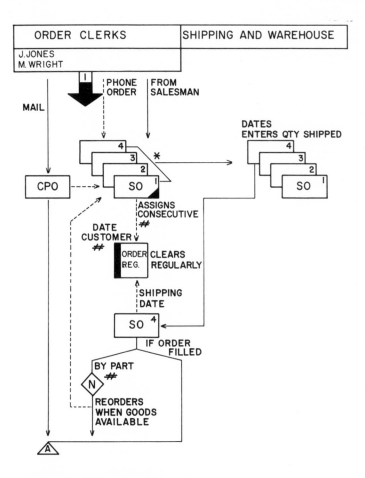

* ORDER CLERKS DETERMINE
CUSTOMER'S SALES TAX STATUS
AND RECORD SAME ON SO

Shipper

The chart below shows the information obtained from the shipper, B. Smith. He initials and dates the sales orders and enters the quantities actually shipped. The first copy is sent as a packing slip with the goods. The second copy is forwarded to the billing clerk. The third copy is used as a delivery copy for in-town orders or as a basis for preparing a bill of lading for out-of-town orders. (In either case the shipper keeps a file by date.)

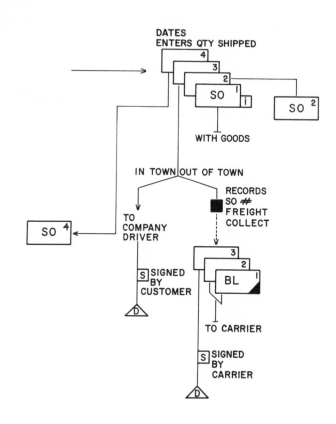

Billing Clerk

The chart below shows the information obtained from the billing clerk, A. Clark. She collects the orders in two- or three-day batches and then prepares four-part prenumbered sales invoices. These are priced from a standard price list with certain agreed discounts for retailers or dealers. The order number is recorded on the invoice and the order is then filed alphabetically. The original copy of the invoice is sent, of course, to the customer. The second, third, and fourth copies are forwarded to the accounts receivable clerk, the inventory records clerk, and the accounting department respectively.

Four-part prenumbered credit notes are distributed in exactly the same way and the billing clerk retains a copy of the supporting documents justifying the credit. (The supporting documents and credit notes are shown below as flowing in from chart B2, for in this particular example the authorization and initiation of credits will be found to be easiest to treat on another chart.)

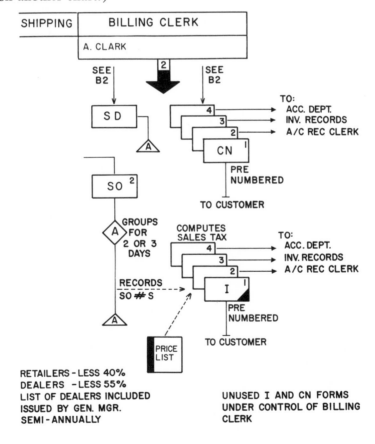

Accounts Receivable Clerk

The chart below shows the information obtained from the accounts receivable clerk, H. Warren. He posts the invoices and credit notes directly to the customer's account card in the accounts receivable ledger, producing the customer's statement at the same time as a carbon copy. The invoices and credit notes are then filed alphabetically. At the end of every month he prepares an aged trial balance in duplicate and forwards the first copy to the comptroller.

BILLING CLERK	ACCOUNTS RECEIVABLE
A. CLARK	H. WARREN

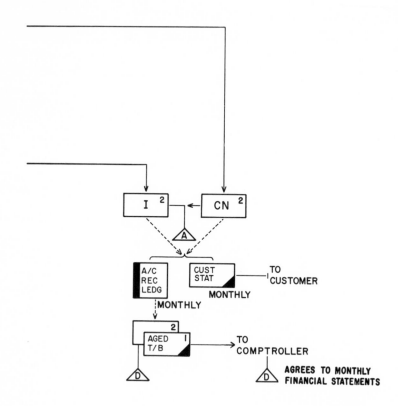

Accounting Clerk

This diagram extends the previous charting to show the additional information obtained from the accounting clerk, T. Walker. He enters the invoices and credit notes in the sales journal (a posting source to the general ledger) and then files them numerically. Periodically he accounts for the numerical continuity of these files.

ACCOUNTS RECEIVABLE	ACCOUNTING CLERK
H. WARREN	T. WALKER

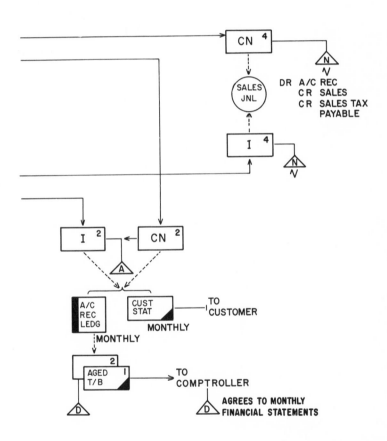

Inventory Records Clerk

The chart below shows the information obtained from the inventory records clerk, S. Brown. He posts the finished goods inventory records (in units only) from the invoices and credit notes and uses the unit standard costs (noted in these records) to cost the invoices and credit notes. He then enters the invoices and credit notes in the cost of sales journal (a posting source to the general ledger) and files them numerically. Periodically he accounts for the numerical continuity of these files.

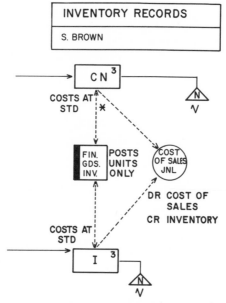

COMPLETE FLOW CHART

The complete flow chart is illustrated in Figure 4. This chart does not, of course, cover credit note initiation, cash sales or cash receipts. In this case it was convenient to cover these procedures on other flow charts. In rare cases it may be possible to show the whole combined system of sales-receivables-receipts on one flow chart. Usually, however, it will be necessary to divide the system into logical components to avoid overcrowding any one chart.

Outline Charts

Flow charts are not intended for skim reading. They are designed for intensive analysis. But with the concentration of information on the average flow chart it is desirable to have some guide to its general content before beginning to read it in detail. Such a purpose can be fulfilled by an outline chart of the type illustrated in Figure 5. The outline chart should have exactly the same column headings as the flow chart (Figure 4), the same starting arrows and concluding circles (posting sources), a line indicating the main path the reader should follow in reading the flow chart, and a bare minimum of words to indicate the major events on the chart ("orders received," "goods shipped," "invoices prepared," etc.). The outline chart should orient the reader by telling him what the flow chart covers before he starts to read it in detail and by keeping him on the right track while he is reading it. It should also assist the charter in detecting any awkwardness or confusion in his flow charts before they are completed. The outline chart is a convenient place to record any apparent weaknesses in control or inefficiences observed in the charted system. This is illustrated in Figure 5, but discussion of these weaknesses and inefficiencies will be deferred until Chapters 5 and 7.

Recording the Systems Audit

In Figure 4 a special section has been laid out as a strip along the bottom of the flow chart. In addition, various numbers and letters have been entered throughout the chart. These represent the mechanics of recording the systems audit performed by the auditor to prove that the system as charted is really in force. The systems audit or walk-through audit is described at length in Chapter 5. However, while on the subject of flow chart preparation here it will be useful to describe this method of recording the systems audit.

In conducting the systems audit the various procedures will have been discussed, of course, with the employees involved. It is useful for the

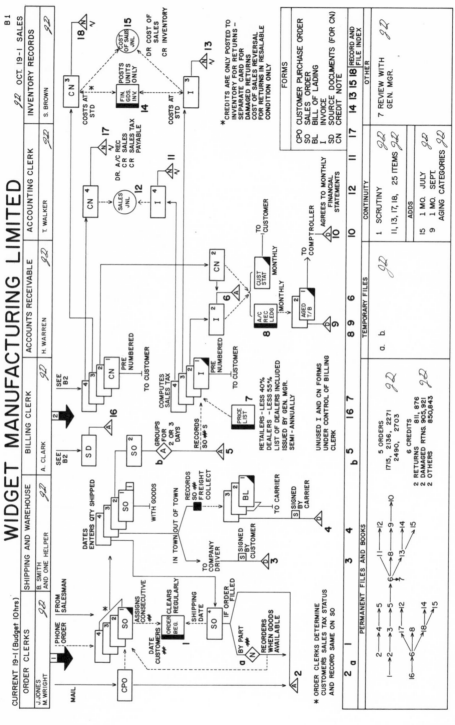

Figure 4. Example of a complete flow chart.

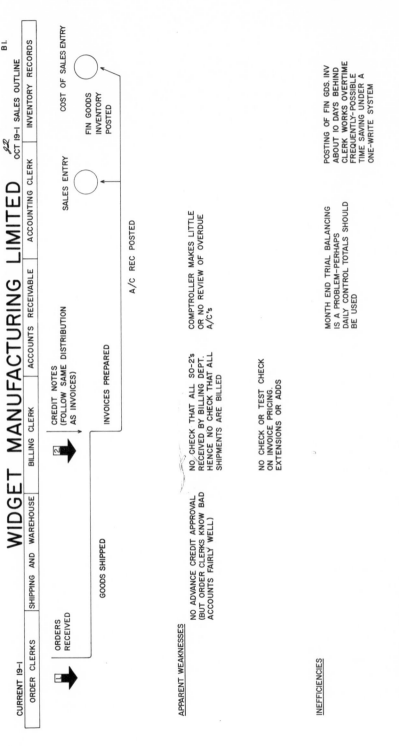

Figure 5. Example of an outline chart.

auditor to indicate that this has been done by initialling beside the appropriate employees' names at the head of each column on the flow charts (as in Figure 4). In this way he can ensure that he has not overlooked any key employee and has in fact obtained the information directly—and not second-hand from employees not involved in a given procedure. As for the record of the actual transactions tested during the systems audit (on the audit strip at the bottom of the flow chart), a system audit *number* is assigned for identification purposes to each book, ledger or permanent file of documents shown on the chart. A systems audit *letter* is assigned to each temporary file of documents.

	Flow chart symbols	*Systems audit numbers and letters*
Books or ledgers, etc.	▮ or ◯	} 1, 2, 3, . . .
Permanent files of documents	△	
Temporary files of documents	◇	a, b, c, . . .

These systems audit numbers and letters are placed (as in Figure 4) below or at the lower corner of the symbol to which they relate. To make it easier to locate particular steps in the audit, the top two lines of the audit strip at the bottom of the flow chart serve as a "record index" showing the horizontal positioning of all the systems audit numbers and letters. Thus, in Figure 4, file number 6 (invoice second copies) is directly above the number 6 in the record index.

The main portion of the systems audit consists of examining and comparing the various permanent files and books while *tracing four transactions along each path of the charted system*. This audit examination and comparision can be described symbolically:

$$1 \rightarrow 2 \rightarrow 3 \rightarrow 4 \rightarrow \ldots \qquad \text{4 orders}$$

The notations in this figure mean that for a sample of four orders, items selected in record 1 were checked to related documents or information in record 2 which in turn were checked to record 3 and thence to record 4, etc.

The interpretation of the basic step

$$1 \rightarrow 2 \qquad \text{4 orders}$$

where 1 and 2 are both files of documents, is that:

(a) Four documents were selected out of file 1.

(b) Each such document was carefully examined and any information or arithmetic which was verifiable without reference to any other source was checked (e.g. extensions, additions, name and address, reasonableness of amount, nature of item, etc.).

(c) If sets of matched documents were contained in file 1 (such as purchase invoices and receiving slips matched and filed together) then four such sets were selected and, in addition to the examination of each document, all common or related information was agreed between the documents of a given set (e.g. receiving date, quantities, descriptions, amounts, etc.).

(d) File 1 was then *scrutinized* briefly to see that it did not contain significant types of transactions not covered on the flow charts and to see that other documents in the file appear to have been processed in the same way as the sample examined.

(e) Then the related documents or sets of documents were located in file 2 and all common or related information agreed between the file 1 documents and the file 2 documents selected.

(f) Then steps (b), (c) and (d) above were carried out for the file 2 documents by themselves.

The systems audit numbers should be assigned in a logical "audit flow order" so that the consecutive numbers represent the consecutive audit steps. In this way the systems audit can really be read without constant cross-reference to the audit strip at the bottom of the chart, since it is known that the steps flow consecutively. Conventionally, a sales audit is conducted in a cradle-to-grave direction (as in Figure 4) while a disbursements audit is conducted in a grave-to-cradle direction. The audit numbers should therefore be assigned accordingly. Occasionally, of course, the systems audit will not lead in a completely straight line, but will appear as follows, say:

$$1 \rightarrow 2 \rightarrow 3 \rightarrow 5 \rightarrow 6 \rightarrow \ldots \ldots$$
$$\downarrow$$
$$4$$

Here, record 3 is checked both to record 4 and to record 5, while 4 cannot be checked to 5 itself. This could occur, for instance, if 3 was a sales invoice, 4 the accounts receivable ledger, and 5 a sales summary. In general, the tracing of transactions from cradle to grave should be done in one continuous chain, as Figure 4 shows. It should not be broken up into segments such as:

$$1 \rightarrow 2 \qquad 2 \rightarrow 3 \qquad 3 \qquad 3 \rightarrow 5 \qquad 5 \rightarrow 6$$
$$\downarrow$$
$$4$$

since this is both slower and less effective than tracing the same transactions throughout the whole path.

When the extent of a particular systems audit is indicated as four items it must be understood that four items will be checked along each segment of the system trail from cradle to grave or from grave to cradle. With a sales audit this is fairly unambiguous: four shipping reports are checked to four invoices that are traced to the sales summary, etc. With a disbursements audit, however, the auditor might select four cheques, where each supporting voucher contains twenty suppliers' invoices and each invoice covers five purchase orders. The intention is not to check four vouchers, eighty invoices, and four hundred purchase orders but rather to check four cheques to the supporting vouchers, four invoices from among these vouchers to purchase orders, four purchase orders from among these invoices to requisitions, etc.

Whenever there is a fork in the system there must be a corresponding set of alternatives in the audit. For example in:

$$1 \rightarrow 2 \rightarrow 3 \rightarrow 5 \rightarrow 6 \rightarrow 7 \qquad \text{4 domestic orders}$$

$$2 \rightarrow 4 \rightarrow 5 \qquad\qquad\qquad \text{4 foreign orders}$$

domestic orders affect record 3 and foreign orders record 4. In this case an additional four transactions should be traced over the alternate path of the variable section (2 to 5) so that every charted path on the flow chart will be covered by the systems audit. It does not matter whether domestic or foreign orders are traced over the rest of the chain (1 to 2 and 5 to 7) as long as four transactions are traced in total. Preferably, the four transactions for the overall path should be selected randomly and then further transactions selected to bring those tested over each branch (2-3-5 and 2-4-5) up to four in number.

The foregoing has dealt with the systems audit relating to permanent files and books—which generally should be the largest part of the systems audit. However, the complete systems audit consists of:
(a) Test and scrutiny of permanent files and books
(b) Test and scrutiny of temporary files
(c) Test of continuity
(d) Test of additions
(e) Other tests (if any).
Sometimes it is possible to trace a chain of related documents in temporary files:

$$a \rightarrow b \rightarrow c \rightarrow d \rightarrow e$$

but more often the checking of related temporary files is likely to be disjointed:

$$a \rightarrow b \qquad e \rightarrow b \qquad h \rightarrow 4$$

However, in any case, all the temporary files should be scrutinized to (a) see that the temporary files are being processed in the way outlined on the flow charts, (b) see if all the items are as current as they should be, and (c) see if any irregular items or problems are accumulating in them.

A check of serial continuity of appropriate files should be made, but for a very limited extent, say twenty-five items. The purpose is merely to see if, at first glance, the client is accounting for continuity and not, at this point, to conduct an extensive audit to detect the occasional missing number. Test adds should be done where appropriate but only to a very limited extent. The purpose is to ascertain the system and not, at this point, to detect the rare manipulation. Often some alternative test may be more appropriate and faster, such as agreeing two independent totals made by different employees in different departments.

Finally, a space is provided in the audit strip for any other audit steps not covered in the above categories. These will occur, say, where an alternative procedure has been described in a footnote and the systems audit of this procedure has not, therefore, been covered in the symbolic description of the main systems audit related to the charts. For each section of the recorded systems audit the auditor's initials can be entered to indicate that he has carried out the program described.

The method outlined for recording the systems audit provides a complete yet concise description of the audit steps performed. In contrast, were all the audit steps to be spelled out in detailed narrative style the systems audit program would become, in effect, a lengthy description of the client's systems. Such a result would be inefficient and would defeat the whole purpose of avoiding lengthy systems narrative by adopting flow charting.

SYMBOLS

☐	Document
◢	Document prepared
[ ]	If copy
⟶	Flow of documents
- - - ➤	Used for next step
⟨	Fork (alternative possibilities)
⊢	Dead-end (leaves charted system)
△A △N △D	Permanent file of documents (alphabetically, numerically, or by date)
△N✓ △N △Nx	Serial continuity checked, unimportant, or unchecked respectively
◇A ◇N ◇D	Temporary file of documents (alphabetically, numerically, or by date)
⊠	Attached
■	Destroyed
⊡	Initials
⊡S	Signs
▐	Book or ledger
◯	Posting source
*	Keyed to explanatory note
⬇1 ⬇2	Starting points

Figure 6. Summary of symbols used.

CHAPTER

5

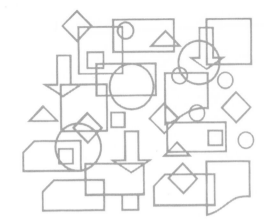

THE SYSTEMS AUDIT

The division of an analytical audit into two stages (systems audit and follow-up audit) has been explained in Chapter 3 and each of these stages discussed in general terms. In Chapter 4 flow charting techniques and the method of recording the systems audit on the flow charts themselves has been described. The various audit procedures constituting the systems audit can now be considered in more detail.

In conducting an analytical audit there are certain obvious differences between a systems audit being made in the initial year (when the flow charts are being prepared for the first time) and one being continued in repeat years (when the flow charts are merely being revised and up-dated). The following pages will describe the procedures primarily in the context of a first-year audit, but reference will be made where necessary to changes appropriate for an audit in repeat years.

Description of Business

Systems analysis must begin with a knowledge of the physical operations of the business being audited. It is too easy to float about in a sea of statements, figures, and journal entries without a grounding in what is really going on in the business. If management sometimes shows signs of exasperation at the sight of new faces among the audit staff, it is because new faces so often mean new minds full of ignorance of what the business is all about. Some might argue that the desired knowledge can be inferred from a careful review of the accounts. This is putting the cart before the horse. It is the propriety of the accounting entries that should be derived from a reasonable knowledge of the business, not vice versa. The intention in preparing or up-dating a description of the client's business (section A) should therefore be to give a bird's-eye view of the physical processes and transactions that underlie the accounting entries and financial statements. The description should tell briefly what the business is and what various factors have an important bearing on its operating results. This section need not be concerned with accounting procedures (which should be covered on the flow charts). Some suggestions of what this description might include are set out below.[1] Not all the specific points mentioned can be determined quickly for every client. Only those points should be covered, of course, where useful information is obtainable and can be summarized in a reasonable amount of time. Finally, this section will only be of use to the auditor as he conducts his systems analysis if he has it in advance. It must therefore be completed before the flow charting begins.[2]

NATURE OF BUSINESS

A one-sentence introduction stating what business the client is in.

OWNERSHIP

One sentence again, stating briefly whether the business is owned privately or publicly, by individuals or by a corporation.

INDUSTRY

Such points as: the nature of the industry (DBS classification); the economic factors affecting the industry (consumer disposable income, etc., competing products, cyclical or seasonal demand); the position of the company in the industry (proportion of total unit sales, number of domestic and foreign competitors, names of major competitors, comparisons with specific competitors, growth potential or outlook).

PLANT FACILITIES

Such points as: the locations and approximate extent of plant, warehouse, and office space, branch locations; whether owned or leased; the age and condition of buildings, room for expansion, present plans for improvement; the nature and extent of equipment (extent of automation, age and condition of machinery); appraisals; capital expenditure budgets; comparisons with competitors.

PRODUCTS

Such points as: description of main product lines, relative volumes, product mix, number of products; the extent of manufacturing in relation to

[1] The suggestions given relate primarily to a manufacturing company but the information appropriate for other types of organization will be analogous.
[2] This point is less critical for internal auditors, who have a closer familiarity with their own organization than the external auditor can hope for without some such aid.

the finished product (and extent of purchases for resale); in which plants the various products are manufactured; service operations; warranty; extent of custom manufacturing versus production for stock; general demand for company's products; plans for new lines, etc.

PRODUCTION

Such points as: the nature of the manufacturing or processing operations; plant capacity; normal operating schedule (peak and slack periods); production planning; storage facilities; engineering program (design, product development, experimental, etc.); research and development budget.

PURCHASING

Such points as: annual volume; main materials purchased; main suppliers and alternate sources; proportion of purchases from affiliated companies; unloading facilities; receiving operations.

PERSONNEL

Such points as: the number of employees (office, warehouse, and plant— average and range from slack to peak periods); union agreements; day work and piece work proportions; average wage rates (comparison with industry if possible); employee benefits, pension plans, etc; strike history and employee relations; employment contracts, bonus plans etc. for senior personnel; organization chart of key personnel.

SALES

Such points as: the method of distribution; the type and number of the company's customers; geographical location of company sales including exports; comparison with industry and specific competitors; sales force, method of remuneration, commissions, bonuses, retainers; seasonal trends; sales promotion and advertising; sales policies; selling and administrative budget; price trends and method of setting prices, proportion of sales to affiliated companies.

OPERATING RESULTS

Such points as: current trends in gross profit and net profit rates; break-even point analysis if available (fixed costs in relation to total costs); comparison of profitability with industry and with specific competitors.

BUDGETING

Such points as: who is in charge of budget preparation; method of sales forecasting; production scheduling, etc.; cash requirements; reports to management (and follow-up of deviations).

SUBSIDIARIES

A very brief outline of any subsidiaries and their operations.

Components of Each Section

Each of sections B to F can conveniently begin with a standard lead sheet, containing a number of reminder questions on internal control. Suggested lead sheets for the different sections are shown in Appendix III. The whole object of the flow charting is to enable the system to be evaluated. The lead sheet is intended to emphasize this purpose. Each lead sheet is divided into four sections: a brief systems summary, an index of the section, a flow charting guide, and the evaluation portion.

The systems summary is intended to be no more than eight to ten lines in point form. It should be a brief resume of the accounting system charted (not the business itself, which is described in section A). The purpose is to help anyone reviewing the working papers and to help next year's audit staff, who will want a brief overall picture before examining the details. The index of the section can record merely the flow chart references (B_1, B_2, etc.) and titles, so that the contents of the section can be seen at a glance. The flow charting guide is a list of different transaction types to remind the auditor of any possible types omitted in error from the flow charts. The evaluation portion of the lead sheet is divided into a number of internal control reminder questions. These reminder questions ask for answers on the key control points in each section; space is also provided for references to the flow charts where the relevant control points can be seen.

The reminder questions are intended to take the place of more extended internal control questionnaires. Questionnaires often produce scores of "not applicable" answers because certain detailed questions, as worded, do not fit exactly the pattern of procedures being reviewed. In theory, the auditor should then think through to the intent of the inappropriate question and rephrase it to apply to the system under examination. In practice, there is a temptation to leave the "not applicable" answer and press on, there being so many pages of questions still awaiting attention. The purpose of the brief reminder questions on the analytical audit lead sheets is to focus attention on the primary control points in each section and thus minimize the risk of perfunctory treatment.

Each lead sheet contains a relatively small number of primary questions such as: "Can goods be shipped but not invoiced?", "Can materials be paid for if not received?", etc. These are the essential control points that must be covered by any adequate system of internal control—although the precise *mechanics* by which they are achieved may vary from system to system. A number of the more usual mechanics of control are listed as secondary points under each primary question. These are only some of many possible ways of achieving the control, however, and the primary control questions are really the more important part of the evaluation section. The subsidiary points are in very abbreviated form and are not intended to substitute for a text book on internal control. Their function is to *remind*, not to *instruct*. As such they make no pretence to be encyclo-paedic—as longer internal control questionnaires can be. The auditor must have a good understanding of normal internal control features (as outlined in numerous texts[3]) before using these lead sheets. He will then find the use of the brief reminder questions coupled with his flow chart analysis to be more efficient and less cumbersome on the actual audit than lengthy questionnaires.[4] The use of the lead sheet questions is discussed more fully in a later part of this chapter.

The lead sheet for each section should be followed by the systems flow charts and (occasionally) any additional systems notes which are required but cannot be incorporated on the flow charts. The standard flow charting technique (as described in Chapter 4) can be used for sections B, C, and D. A discussion of the points peculiar to each of these sections is included in Chapter 7. The cost section (E) should include both a flow chart of the procedural flow and a schedule summarizing the cost entries. The former can be a standard flow chart—though usually with more narrative ex-planations and footnotes than in other sections. The latter should outline the logic of the cost accounting system: the skeleton entries (whether from sections B, C, D, or E) which form the basis for the flow of costs through inventory into cost of sales. Examples of both are given in Chapter 7. Section F, summarizing the flow of information from all the posting sources into the general ledger, requires a different type of chart, which is also illustrated in Chapter 7. Any additional description of journal entries, etc. not previously covered should normally be in narrative point form. This section should also summarize the flow of information from the accounts into the monthly statements or other periodic management re-ports (this summarization can usually be in narrative point form).

Flow Charting and the Systems Audit

In beginning the systems review of a particular section (such as sales-

---

[3]As, for example, *Montgomery's Auditing*, 8th ed. 1957, an excellent authority on internal con-trol, among other subjects.

[4]Preferences will obviously vary on this point. Each method has its advantages and disadvantages and many practitioners may well continue to favour the more expanded questionnaire.

receivables-receipts) the auditor must first obtain a general idea of what is included in that section. This can be done by (a) reading the description of the business (section A) to see what types of transactions should be expected; (b) discussing the overall system briefly with the comptroller or chief accountant; and (c) reviewing any accounting manual, procedure books, comptroller's circulars, and systems department memoranda outlining the system. Detail in these preliminary steps must be avoided. Information from (b) and (c) may be out of date. In any case it represents what senior officials think is happening or should be happening; the actual system in operation may be considerably different.[5] (In repeat years, the auditor should review the previous year's flow charts for the given section and discuss any subsequent changes briefly with the comptroller or chief accountant.) This preliminary information is to be used for orientation. It should show where the careful systems review can logically begin. The preliminary information is usually best recorded in the form of a rough flow chart, which can be added to and amended during the course of the systems audit. It should not be charted in elaborate detail, since extensive corrections are almost certain to be required.

The next step is to read the internal control questions on the related lead sheet. These are the questions for which the charts will have to furnish the answers. The answers cannot, of course, be given as yet but the questions should serve as a *guide* in the actual charting. Procedures having a bearing on basic control points will have to be charted in sufficient detail to ensure that the control is accurately described. Procedures having little or no bearing on control should be charted with a lesser degree of detail or omitted entirely—at least, as far as external auditors are concerned. It must be remembered, however, that not all control procedures are located within the accounting department. Many procedures performed by other departments—perhaps "administrative controls" aimed primarily at promoting efficiency—may provide some important check on the accuracy or reliability of the accounting system.[6] In repeat years the auditor must

[5]The internal auditor, however, may wish to flow chart all standard procedures laid down in company manuals and then measure all deviations from these prescribed procedures encountered during his systems audit.

[6]It is common to divide internal control into *accounting controls*, which safeguard assets and accounting reliability (some would subdivide this further into *internal check* and *accounting controls*), and *administrative controls*, which promote operational efficiency. Some administrative controls may have little effect on the accounting reliability; others may compensate for deficient accounting controls and thus have a very important effect. In this book all the controls are referred to under the generic term, "internal control." Any procedure which provides a significant check on the accounting reliability or on the safeguarding of assets (whether direct or indirect, whether an accounting or an administrative control) should be covered in the auditor's review and recorded on his flow charts.

review the answers given on the previous year's lead sheets since these will indicate where particular attention should be focussed during the current year's review. He should also review the disposition of recommendations made to the client in the previous year. Adopted suggestions will necessitate flow chart revisions. Unadopted ones may require further investigation to locate any apparent obstacles to their implementation.

Bearing in mind these internal control points, the auditor should then begin at the "cradle" and trace through to the "grave" (or vice versa) for each type of transaction. In tracing each transaction he should discuss the procedures with the employee who performs them. That is, he should ask A rather than accept B's assertion as to what A does. As he questions each employee with respect to the transaction being traced, he should ask what that employee's procedures are, what books he keeps, what documents he processes, from whom he receives them, and to whom he sends them. In repeat years the employees need not be questioned as fully as in the first-year analytical audit. All employees, however, must still be questioned *briefly* to confirm that the previous year's system is still in force or to discover the extent of any changes. If this inquiry is combined with questions concerning the particular sample of transactions being traced, the necessary review can be completed without giving the impression of repeating the "first-year" survey all over again.

The information obtained during the systems review should be taken down in *flow chart form,* but on a rough chart. Half the benefit is lost if the auditor records his interview in narrative and then subsequently sits down to translate this narrative into flow chart form. Flow charting is faster right from the start because it is a form of shorthand. It also helps the auditor to *visualize* the system under review and to see immediately what loose ends have been left unexplained. Covering the system thoroughly with a given employee the first time will save many repeat visits to the same employee to clarify the information obtained initially. On the other hand, it is wise not to try to follow too many parts of the system at once. Where one employee is involved in several stages of the system it may be simplest to trace the stages chronologically even if it means coming back to the same employee for a subsequent stage. For instance, in reviewing sales order procedures the auditor might want to defer consideration of back orders until the normal orders were covered completely. Discussion with each employee must therefore be directed to the subject at hand and prevented from wandering into extraneous subjects, excessive detail, or procedures better deferred temporarily. This requires both organization and tact; but if it is neglected much time can be wasted.

It is essential, then, that the *direction* and *degree of detail* of the systems review be controlled at all times. The course of the review must not dart aimlessly from department to department in any direction suggested by the latest answer received. This would lead to sprawling, disorganized flow charts. The rough preliminary chart obtained from talking to the comptroller or chief accountant should give a good indication in advance of what each flow chart should cover if it is to relate to other charts in an orderly manner. The degree of detail must also be kept commensurate with the importance of the point being charted. *The single, most serious danger to avoid is the laborious charting of unnecessary detail.* Where internal control is not directly involved, a certain amount of *simplification* is essential.

On smaller engagements (and on all engagements in repeat years) the most efficient method usually is to conduct the systems audit simultaneously with the systems review. That is, the documents and records relating to four or five transactions of each type being charted should be checked and compared when the staff member is first discussing the procedures with the employees involved. This completes the whole job in one "walkthrough" rather than two. On larger engagements in the first year it may sometimes be too complicated to conduct the systems audit simultaneously with the systems review. In these cases the systems review and *rough* flow charts can be made simultaneously and then the cradle-to-grave systems audit performed to verify the rough charts. Here the systems audit is likely to disclose various inaccuracies; these can be corrected on the rough charts. What must be avoided, however, is the preparing of final, neat charts prior to the systems audit; they would almost certainly have to be recharted when the systems audit was done.

Whatever the timing of the systems audit, the auditor must ensure that it establishes the accuracy of *every path* included on the flow chart. For sections B to E the systems audit is divided into the following components: (a) test and scrutiny of permanent files and books, (b) test and scrutiny of temporary files, (c) test of continuity, (d) test of additions, (e) other tests. For section F the systems audit consists of: (a) test of postings, (b) test of additions in general ledger accounts, (c) clearing of opening entries and testing of the trial balance (which can be combined with scrutiny of the general ledger), (d) test of any journal entries not covered in prior sections, (e) test of the building up of general ledger accounts to monthly statements. The technique of recording the systems audit has already been described in Chapter 4.

In the analytical approach it is important that the auditor trace *all* related document copies that have a bearing on the reliability of the system. He should not skip directly, for instance, from the first shipping order copy to the last posting in the accounts receivable records. The purpose of the systems-oriented audit is not just to verify the completion of the small sample of transactions checked but to establish the mechanics of the system—including all important intermediate steps. Thus his reliance on the sales system would be based not just on the ultimate posting of the few shipments tested but on his knowledge of the processing, recording, matching, and reconciling of other shipping order copies, other sales invoice copies, the bill of lading, various numerical registers or listings, etc. The significant intermediate steps must therefore be traced in the systems audit and included on the systems flow charts.

Another important step is to establish that the rough charts have in fact covered *all the possible types* of transactions occurring in the system. It is essential that all parts of the system be covered so that they will be (1) checked during the systems audit and (2) evaluated from a control point of view. Therefore, the auditor should look to see if any relevant transactions described or implied in the description of the business (section A) do not appear in the accounting system charted. Secondly, while the systems audit is being done he must *scrutinize the books, ledgers, and document files* carefully for types of transactions not covered as yet on the charts or in the audit. Thirdly, he should refer to the flow charting guide on the sectional lead sheets for possible variations in transaction type, and ensure by scrutiny of records and questioning of employees that all variations occurring have been covered. In repeat years there will not be the same risk that the chart has omitted any type of transaction. Nonetheless, the auditor should review section A and the charting guide on the lead sheet and consider whether any change in the current year has resulted in new types of transactions which must be added to the charts.

There may be a few types of transactions which occur so infrequently during the year that no regular, laid-down, and verifiable system can be said to exist for them. If material, these must be noted so that they can be followed up specifically during the year-end visit. The auditor should also enquire about procedures during slack periods, peak periods, vacations, illnesses, coffee breaks, etc. It is usually not convenient to chart all these variables on the flow charts, but they should be investigated since a marked deviation from the normal routine or division of duties as charted might have a significant effect on the internal control.

Finally, it might be noted that extended procedures such as detailed cash counts, attendance at pay distributions and verification of *all* items on one bank reconciliation are not necessary in the systems audit. These extended procedures will occur occasionally in the weakness investigation (but only where they are necessary to cover specific weaknesses in the system) and they will occur periodically (on a cyclical basis) among the supplementary tests. It would be inconsistent, however, with the whole basis of allocating audit effort based on a study of internal control to include these extended procedures automatically in the systems audit.

Final Flow Charts

When the systems audit has been completed and the rough charts are known to represent the system actually in force, the final flow charts can be prepared neatly on standard charting paper with the aid of standard templates. The final charts must be made *readable* for others. It is not enough for the flow charts to be accurate; they must be understandable to a reviewer and to a new staff member next year. They must be clear, concise, logically organized and unambiguous. It is unlikely that a neat recopying of the rough charts will, by itself, satisfy these conditions. Some reorganizing will be necessary. Methods of improving flow charts are considered in Chapter 8.

In repeat years it may be necessary to modify the previous year's final flow charts based on the information obtained in the current year's systems audit. This will usually involve erasing obsolete sections of the previous year's chart, erasing the preliminary indication of changes noted on the chart during the systems audit, and recharting the revised part of the chart appropriately. The audit description at the bottom of the flow chart and the layout of the outline chart must both be revised, of course, to correspond to any systems changes charted. Where systems changes are extensive, or where a series of patches over successive years have gradually complicated a flow chart unduly, it will sometimes be simpler to redraw a fresh final chart. Usually, the previous chart will be helpful as a guide in drawing the new chart. A brief reference to any significant systems changes which have occurred since last year can also be made on the outline charts. A full description is not needed. The point of the reference is to highlight areas where possible strengthening or weakening of control may have resulted.

After each detailed flow chart is completed, the auditor should prepare the related outline chart to orient the reader and facilitate review. The outline chart has been described in Chapter 4. A convenient arrangement for filing these working papers is to have the outline chart on the back of the preceding (i.e. facing) page. In this way both the detailed flow chart and the related outline chart can be viewed together.

Volume Summary

The flow charts indicate the *design* of the system but they do not show the physical *volume* of accounting work. Yet in assessing internal control and efficiency the auditor must be able to see the different procedures in perspective. It is therefore useful to summarize such data as the number of customers, products, inventory accounts, etc., and the monthly volumes of cheques, vouchers, purchase invoices, sales invoices, shipping orders, credit notes, journal entries, etc. A more detailed list of the volume statistics which might be considered for incorporation in this summary is as follows (although only a selection of these would probably be appropriate in any individual case):

Section	*Monthly volumes of*	*Total number of*
B	sales orders	customers – active accounts
	sales invoices	customers – inactive accounts
	shipments	customers – by category
	units shipped	salesmen
	back orders	order clerks
	credit notes	billing clerks
	cheques received	accounts receivable clerks
	accounts receivable postings	
	cash sales slips	
C	purchase requisitions	purchasing department
	purchase orders	employees
	purchase invoices	
	receiving slips	
	suppliers' debits	
	vouchers	
	cheques issued	
D	daily work tickets	office employees
	payroll cheques	(monthly, semi-monthly)
	piece work tickets	plant employees (weekly)
		(range and peaks during year)
		employees by category
		or by location
		payroll department employees

E	production orders	products
	units produced	manufactured parts,
	production change notices	sub-assemblies
	scrap reports	inventory accounts
	perpetual inventory	(by category)
	postings	cost ledger accounts
	cost ledger postings	cost department employees
F	journal entries	general ledger accounts
	general ledger postings	accounting department
		employees

Comparative figures can be added in subsequent years so that any marked trends in the volume of accounting work will be evident.

Evaluation of Internal Control

Where an audit staff of more than one is involved on an analytical audit, it is important that the evaluation of the internal control for a section be done by the staff member who charted or up-dated the section. If he is using sectional lead sheets of the type suggested in Appendix III he should answer the primary internal control questions and indicate, in the spaces provided, the references to the flow charts where the answers to these primary control questions are supported. The evaluation of the internal control should be made by (a) reviewing the flow charts themselves (looking for inappropriate divisions of duties or lack of automatic checks, etc.), and (b) reviewing the internal control reminder questions on the lead sheet; and (c) in repeat years, considering weaknesses noted in the past to see if they are still present.

In analyzing the flow charts for internal control it is useful to ask with respect to each step in the system:

What would happen if this one step were omitted or performed incorrectly, either by accident or by intent? Would the omission or error be detected automatically by the system?

If it would be detected, the internal control is satisfactory. If not, it is weak. For instance, if a sales invoice copy is normally matched to a shipping order copy, then failure to prepare an invoice would be detected by an unmatched shipping order. In effect, the system contains two paths leading to the "destination"—in this case, the *place* of matching. If either path to the destination fails, its failure will be detected by the other. Only if both failed simultaneously—which can be dismissed as too improbable provided the two paths are really *independent*—would the error go undetected. While the circumstances are varied in practice, most elements of internal control consist of some form of *two independent paths to the same "destination."*

Consider, for example, the system illustrated in Figure 4. It can be seen that if (a) Walker's invoice copy is not entered in the sales journal, then (b) Warren's copy, when posted to the accounts receivable ledger, will cause a balancing difference which in turn should lead to detection of the error. On the other hand, if (a) Warren never receives his invoice copy, then (b) Walker's copy, when entered in the sales journal, will cause a balancing difference which in turn should lead to detection of the error. Finally, if (a) both copies of the invoice are lost together just after preparation, then (b) Walker would notice the missing invoice number and hence detect the error. Thus, whatever one single step is omitted or performed incorrectly some other step in the system catches the omission or error automatically. Therefore, to the lead sheet question: "Can sales be invoiced but not recorded in the accounts?" the answer (barring collusion) is no. Internal control on this point appears satisfactory.

The characteristics of a satisfactory system of internal control include: (a) the delegation to specific individuals of powers of approval and the institution of checks to see that transactions are approved by authorized individuals; (b) a division of record keeping so that one record is checked by another record created independently; (c) proper physical control of assets, including dual custody of valuable negotiable assets; (d) separation of the custody of assets from the recording of the same assets and related transactions; (e) periodic verification of the existence of the recorded assets; and (f) employment of personnel having abilities and training commensurate with their responsibilities. Of these elements of internal control, (a), (b), (d) and (e) should be able to be seen from the flow charts themselves. Objective (c), and sometimes (d), is not as readily determinable from the charts, but the auditor should have observed its presence or absence when preparing the flow charts and conducting the systems audit. Objective (f), finally, cannot be determined from the flow charts: a system may be *structurally* good but fail because of incompetent personnel. Therefore, it is an important part of the auditor's job during the systems audit to form some opinion as to the competence of the employees involved—at least, in those areas where it has a bearing on the effectiveness of the system of internal control. In summary, apparent weaknesses to be determined during this phase of the audit may be (1) *structural* weaknesses reflecting poor systems design or inappropriate division of duties, etc., or (2) *inadequate physical control* of assets observed by the auditor in the course of gathering information for his flow charts, or (3) *incompetent personnel* observed by the auditor or evidenced by the number of errors occurring (though subsequently detected) in the system.

When all apparent weaknesses in internal control have been determined they should be described concisely on the appropriate outline charts. The note of the weakness on the outline chart should appear in the same column as that in which the weakness may actually be seen on the facing flow chart. This is to emphasize the relationship of the control evaluation to the flow charts drawn and to make it easier for a reviewer to examine the reported weakness on the flow chart. Occasionally, of course, where the weakness relates to several areas, the choice of column will have to be arbitrary. The weakness should, in any case, be described in terms applicable to the particular system. These may well differ from the phrasing of the question on the lead sheet. The point of the reminder questions on the lead sheet is not to regiment the expression of the conclusions but only to ensure that nothing has been overlooked. Weaknesses must of course be noted, even in cases where they are impractical to cure. The mere fact that a particular weakness in a given business may not be worth the cost of correction does not mean that the auditor can ignore it in his audit.

In repeat years, weaknesses should be recorded by revising the previous year's description of the apparent weaknesses on the outline charts where appropriate and adding any new weaknesses encountered in the current year.

Observations on Efficiency

In the course of the above review of the flow charts to evaluate internal control, the auditor should be alert for any apparent inefficiencies in the system. These may include unnecessary handling of certain documents, inefficient routing of certain documents, unnecessary document copies or records or unused information thereon, inadequate planning or delegation of work, inadequate instructions to employees, insufficient or excessive office machinery, poor utilization of data processing facilities, poorly planned reports, bad work scheduling, lack of employee incentive, or inefficient office layout. All apparent inefficiencies should be described concisely on the appropriate outline charts. The note of the inefficiency on the outline chart should again appear in the same column as that in which the inefficiency may actually be seen on the facing flow chart. Occasionally, of course, the choice of column will be arbitrary.

No formal questionnaire is suggested for the auditor to complete in order to evaluate efficiency, since this represents a collateral service rather than the primary objective of the audit.[7] He must watch at all times for inefficiencies or areas where improvements could be made but consider these as a free by-product from the flow charting required to evaluate the internal control. The flow charting should itself be aimed at control and not specifically at efficiency evaluation.

Scrutiny

Following the flow chart review the auditor should scrutinize such books of account, other records, and statements as practical for the year to date. This is in addition to the scrutiny of document files which should have been done during the actual cradle-to-grave audit. What is practical to scrutinize is, of course, a question of judgment. An accounting record in which unusual or irregular transactions or entries could be noticed easily, if they occurred, is usually worth scrutinizing. One in which unusual entries would be particularly hard to differentiate from routine entries is probably not worth scrutinizing. If the books of original entry are cumbersome to scrutinize, a careful scrutiny of all general ledger accounts may accomplish the same end more efficiently. If the general ledger accounts (such as the cost accounts) are vast in number, a careful scrutiny of monthly statements or other management reports may be more effective. Sometimes, it may be appropriate to scrutinize a drawerful of invoices or a file of the year's bank reconciliations. It depends on the type of records and statements involved.

When scrutinizing a book or record the auditor should be watching for miscellaneous and unusual transactions which require explanation, or which suggest accounting errors, or which should arouse suspicion of fraud, or which require specific verification because they are not part of the regular system charted. He should *also* be alert for recurring transactions of a type which are not yet, but should be, covered on his flow charts. The scrutiny of the general ledger is a convenient time for the auditor to clear all opening entries to the prior year's balance sheet file and to check (or test check) the monthly trial balancing of the general ledger.

Internal Audit Department

Where an internal audit department exists a new element of control is added, which the external auditor is entitled to take into account in designing his audit. The scope of the internal audit function can vary from one employee occasionally checking some petty cash funds to a fully organized

[7]A formal questionnaire on efficiency points may, however, be desirable for internal auditors.

department covering all phases of the client's operations. The internal audit function may be directed solely to branch locations or it may cover the client's head office procedures as well. The external auditor should first, therefore, determine the scope of the internal audit. Then he can consider the department's independence, to whom they report, their competence, the amount of training given, the amount of laid-down audit instructions or programs, the frequency of reporting and the quality of their reports. His findings and conclusions should be summarized and included in his working papers.

After this general assessment, the internal audit procedures should be reviewed in more detail to see to what extent the external auditor may rely on this work and reduce his tests accordingly. He should review the internal audit reports for confirmation of his conclusions on apparent weaknesses or for indications of any additional weak areas. Based on this, he may have to revise his notes of apparent weaknesses to allow for the extent to which previously noted weaknesses are offset by internal audit procedures or, conversely, to incorporate additional weaknesses uncovered by the internal auditors. Finally, it is axiomatic that great gains in efficiency can be achieved if there is close cooperation between internal and external auditors. The external auditor should consider the extent to which his work can be coordinated with that of the internal auditors. He might examine the possibility of joint use of his flow charts or the possibility of *the internal auditors up-dating the flow charts throughout the year*. It is particularly convenient, of course, if both internal and external auditors are using the same analytical auditing approach.

Weakness Follow-up Sheet

Once the apparent weaknesses have been determined and are noted on the outline charts throughout the file the auditor must decide what he is going to do about them. It is useful to summarize these decisions in one place. A convenient way is on a weakness follow-up sheet of the type shown in Figure 7. This schedule represents a complete record of all apparent weaknesses in control discovered during the systems audit visit. (A new weakness follow-up sheet should be prepared each year but it may be useful to retain the schedules for a few immediately preceding years in the file for reference.) For each weakness recorded, the schedule should state the kind of error which might occur (and remain undetected) because of the apparent deficiency in control. This is an essential intermediate step. A suitable audit program cannot be devised to compensate for a weakness unless it is first decided what one is looking for. Moreover, it would be foolish to waste a major audit investigation looking for

"X" COMPANY LIMITED

CURRENT 19–1   JH   DEC. 19–1   WEAKNESS FOLLOW-UP

Chart reference	Weakness	Could material errors occur?	Weakness investigation Description	Initial	Results	Revision to balance sheet program
B₁	No advance credit approval	Could run up large accounts with doubtful risks.	No detailed audit but reviewed to see if any apparent accumulation of bad accounts.	JH	Slight increase in overdue accounts but no specific problems apparent as yet.	Emphasize verification of allowance for doubtful accounts.
B₁	Keypunching of special, non-standard prices not checked	Non-standard prices account for 10% of total sales value. A high frequency of errors could be material but a limited frequency would not be significant.	Examined 120 non-standard invoices (10 per month) and checked to price list.	JH	1 small error found (invoice #23691). Due to carelessness. Decided frequency of such errors must be well under, say, 5% of non-standard sales (e.g. ½% of total sales) and hence could not be material in total.	None
B₁	Lost sales order (after shipping) would not be detected	Material amount of unbilled shipments might occur.	None. (More efficient to add year-end test)	—	—	Check client's annual year-end tab listing of outstanding order cards and trace to sales control orders and to order register.
B₁	Shipping area not guarded and is accessible to outsiders	Inventory is high bulk low value. Material amount of theft would be noticed.	None	—	—	None
C₂	Suppliers' statements not reconciled on a regular basis	Significant errors in accounts payable could go uncorrected.	Examined 10 larger and 30 smaller suppliers' statements and reconciled to accounts payable.	JH	15 branch purchase invoices not set up although 2 months old. Many discrepancies on reconciliation of debit and credit notes. See details on 5b. 10 of missing invoices subsequently found in inventory records (misfiled); copies of other 5 obtained from supplier.	Unless (a) statement reconciliation is instituted (as recommended) and (b) inventory record processing revised prior to year-end, extend accounts payable confirmation and statement reconciliation work at year-end to cover larger proportion of accounts.
D₁	Check of work tickets for piece work to production records not adequate	Significant overbooking of direct labour could occur.	Analyzed labour variance for 7 months to date.	JH	All but $4,000 of the total variance can be accounted for (see 5c) in terms of wage rate increase. Decided any overbooking could not therefore be material in amount.	None

Figure 7. Weakness follow-up sheet.

minor errors or, conversely, rely on a minor audit step to detect major errors. Therefore, the auditor must decide not only the kind but also the seriousness of the error for which he is looking. In some cases the auditor can decide that although errors could occur owing to a given weakness, none of them could be material. In other cases the errors could, perhaps, become material, but only if there were a very high frequency of them. In still other cases even a low frequency of errors might represent a material total.

Next, the auditor must decide what is to be done about each weakness recorded. There are the following alternatives. First, he can decide to do nothing—if it has been decided that no *material* errors could occur anyway.[8] Secondly, he can plan to revise the nature, timing, or extent of certain balance sheet audit procedures. This would be logical if the revised procedure can by itself provide adequate assurance that no material error has occurred and if this is a more efficient way of gaining such assurance than any additional current audit step. Thirdly, he can plan a *weakness investigation* to be carried out during the follow-up visit of the analytical audit. This would be logical if the investigation can by itself provide adequate assurance that no material error has occurred and if this is a more efficient way of gaining this assurance than any revision to the balance sheet audit program. Fourthly, he can do both a balance sheet audit revision and a weakness investigation. This would be logical if neither is sufficient by itself but together they can provide adequate assurance that no material error has occurred, or if this combination is more efficient than either separately.

Where a weakness investigation has been planned, the planned program can be described on the weakness follow-up sheet. Where a revision to the normal balance sheet program has been planned, the proposed revision can also be noted. The remainder of the schedule, of course, is left blank until the weakness investigation is actually carried out during the follow-up audit. (Figure 7 represents the case where the follow-up audit has been completed.) Sometimes it is also useful to indicate on this schedule any internal audit work which has a bearing on the weakness.

There are two reasons for drafting the weakness investigation during the systems audit visit but deferring execution of it until the follow-up audit visit. First, the systems audit is the logical time to design the required investigation because it is at this point that the auditor has the greatest amount of systems knowledge fresh in his mind. In fact, the steps of reviewing the system, analyzing the weaknesses, and deciding what

[8]However, internal auditors may wish to carry out some investigation even when the errors could not be material.

investigation should be done on their account are really one continuous process—and should be done together at the same time. However, the systems audit visit may be relatively early in the fiscal year, which is not the best time to carry out the actual weakness investigation. The point of the investigation is to prove that no material errors (whether innocent or fraudulent) have occurred in an area where internal control cannot itself be relied upon to prevent them. Naturally, the auditor wants to have this assurance for the year as a whole. Because the control is weak, the fact that no material errors are found during the first three months cannot be taken as an indication that the last nine months are equally error-free. When there is a hole in the net the fish which did not escape a minute ago can still escape now. Therefore, the auditor must schedule his weakness investigation for later in the year when the major portion of the year's results are open to review and testing. This, of course, is the point of having a separate follow-up audit visit.

The second reason for deferring execution of the weakness investigation is that it provides an opportunity between the systems audit and the follow-up audit for review and for more senior judgment to be brought to bear. For sole practitioners working without assistants this point is irrelevant. But for any auditors who work in a team or delegate certain work to subordinates, proper review of the audit work performed is a very important consideration. Forming conclusions on the apparent weaknesses discovered and deciding what should be done about them is the area involving the greatest use of judgment. It is therefore this area which will most benefit from the application of more mature judgment and greater experience. If such judgment should lead to modifications in the weakness investigation initially planned, it is desirable that these modifications be made before the investigation is carried out rather than afterwards. For this reason the most important review should fall between the systems audit and the follow-up audit.

There are two exceptions to the above rules. First, where circumstances are encountered which arouse definite suspicions of fraud (as opposed to observed weaknesses which merely permit the possibility of error but do not particularly suggest its existence) then the auditor has a duty to resolve his doubts immediately and not wait for the follow-up visit. In such cases, then, the auditor must carry out *at once* whatever audit investigation is considered necessary to satisfy these doubts. Secondly, in some cases where no weakness investigation is called for (either because errors could not be material or because revised balance sheet procedures are being planned instead) the auditor may still decide on some small amount of checking during the follow-up visit, solely for the purpose of strengthening a recommendation to the client. For instance, he may want to be able to quote an example of errors permitted by the present system to illustrate the problem for which a solution is being proposed. In such cases the follow-up work is not directed at the primary objective of an audit opinion but at the discretionary work to provide collateral services to the client. It is important to realize this so that the test can be stopped as soon as sufficient information is acquired to provide the service.

Draft Weakness Investigation

In drafting a proposed weakness investigation for approval the auditor should remember the following points. The purpose is not to see whether any errors are occurring at all but whether any *material amount* of error has occurred over the year. The weakness investigation may, but it *need not always*, be an extended procedural test—that is, the checking of a larger sample of sales invoices, cancelled cheques, purchase invoices, or other documents. Many times such checking would only detect a few minor errors and still leave unanswered the question of whether any *material amount* of error had occurred over the year. Instead, the weakness investigation may often consist of:
(1) Analysis of certain variance accounts; or
(2) Analysis of budget performance of certain items; or
(3) More intensive scrutiny of certain records; or
(4) Reconciliation of certain operating statistics; or
(5) Further questioning of certain employees; or
(6) Examination of larger documents only, for the entire year; or
(7) Any other appropriate steps that can be devised.
It is, in other words, up to the ingenuity of the auditor to devise the investigation which has the best chance of detecting any errors *material enough to distort the financial statements* should they occur. No set verification steps can be specified in advance, and extended procedural tests will not always be the best answer.

The investigation must naturally relate to the specific weakness and must be assured of detecting any significant errors if, in fact, they occurred. For instance, checking the billing copy of the shipping order to the accounts receivable copy of the sales invoice would not prove that goods shipped were billed if, say, the particular weakness being checked were that the billing copy of the shipping order might have been lost en route to the billing department. (The problem here, of course, could be solved by checking from a shipping order copy retained in the shipping department, or else accounting for continuity of shipping order numbers in the billing department.)

To give one further example of a weakness investigation, consider a case where there is little control to ensure that everything shipped is billed, owing to the lack of cross-reference of order and invoice copies. One could check a large sample of shipping orders (appropriate copies, that is) to the sales invoices. This, however, might be very time-consuming, owing to the system of filing. (In fact the system of filing is probably a contributing cause of the weakness.) Thus, a check of ten shipping reports (two hours work) might reveal one for which no sales invoice could be found. A check of one hundred shipping reports (two days work) might reveal seven for which invoices could not be located. So far, the seven apparent errors found might all be small—but would they be so for the other thousand shipments for the month or the twelve thousand for the year? A 7% failure-to-bill rate would be catastrophic, so the auditor cannot accept this uncertainty. On the other hand, expanding his time-consuming test only to find, as suspected, six or seven out of every hundred invoices cannot be found would be costly without being conclusive. An alternative might be to select a statistical sample of invoices for the year and compare the mean mark-up for the sample with the gross profit on the annual statements (after inventory adjustments). This could at least establish whether any *material dollar value* of unbilled shipments had occurred during the year. This particular test may not always be appropriate or economical but it serves as an example of the alternative to procedural testing. *When a procedure is obviously weak the repeated checking of details of it over and over again is of little value.* Some other approach may, in less time, give a better answer to the question of whether a material amount of error has occurred.

In those cases, however, where extended procedural tests are appropriate to employ in the weakness investigation, the sample of transactions or documents selected for examination should generally be drawn *randomly from the whole year* rather than as a block in one month. It is impossible, of course, to select from the whole year until after the year-end but the goal can be approximated by scheduling the follow-up visit late in the year when most of the year's results are available for audit. (This is in contrast to the systems audit visit, which can be scheduled early in the year.)

The extent of the weakness investigation may be reduced where reliance can be placed on the procedures of the internal audit department. This should only be done, however, where the latter procedures really provide some assurance that no material errors have occurred during the year. Where the results of the internal audit program merely reveal the existence of a weakness without assessing the extent of any errors it may have allowed, then there are no grounds for the external auditor to reduce his weakness investigation.

An example of a weakness follow-up sheet has already been referred to in Figure 7. Six different weaknesses were noted in this case. One of the six weaknesses was judged immaterial. Of the other five, one was scheduled for treatment in the balance sheet audit alone, two were dealt with in the analytical (follow-up visit) alone, and two involved both analytical audit and balance sheet audit work. Of the steps performed during the weakness investigation it will be noticed that some involved checking samples of documents, such as the invoice pricing and the suppliers' statements, while other involved non-procedural tests, such as analyzing the labour variances. (Certain of the results found required elaboration on pages 5b and 5c which would have followed this schedule.) The different weaknesses and audit steps illustrated on this follow-up sheet are not necessarily "average" for the normal audit but merely show some of the types which might arise. The seriousness of the same weakness can vary substantially between two different businesses and the audit steps proposed in this example might be either insufficient or excessive in other circumstances.

Revised Balance Sheet Program

It has been stated earlier that weaknesses discovered in the system may call not only for a weakness investigation during the analytical audit but also (in the case of external auditors) for a revision of the balance sheet audit program as well. In drafting a proposed revision to the balance sheet audit program there are four alternatives. First, the auditor may decide to increase the extent or thoroughness of some regular balance sheet audit procedure. For instance, if one weakness is the absence of any proper credit control procedures, then the risk is that the client may accumulate a large number of doubtful accounts. The best audit for this weakness may be to increase the thoroughness of the year-end verification of the allowance for doubtful accounts. (Of course, some preliminary work earlier in the year may still be advisable to gauge the magnitude of the problem.)

Secondly, the auditor may decide to change the timing of some regular balance sheet audit procedure to the year-end. For instance, if there is poor segregation of cash and accounts receivable and every possibility for serious "lapping" it may be necessary to confirm accounts receivable and verify cash together at the year-end rather than at any earlier date. Thirdly, the auditor may add some separate procedure to the balance sheet audit program to cover the weakness specifically. For instance, the audit of a special year-end reconciliation made by the client of orders received, orders shipped, and orders billed may provide adequate assurance that there were no large unbilled shipments for the year. In this case the year-end test might be far more efficient than any test which could be directed at this weakness during the analytical audit. Fourthly, the auditor may use a combination of some or all of the above three alternatives. The choice of the right alternative will depend upon the nature of the weakness and of the errors which might occur on its account. The same principles apply as for the weakness investigation during the analytical audit. A weakness investigation and a special revision of the balance sheet audit program are merely two different methods of accomplishing the same thing.

Proposed Supplementary Tests

Even when the weaknesses have been covered by planned weakness investigations or by revised balance sheet steps, it is desirable to do some further work to support (on a test basis) the conclusion that control in other areas is satisfactory. A convenient plan is to select one or two supplementary tests from each section of the system: sales-receivables-receipts (B), purchases-payables-payments (C), payrolls (D), cost records (E), etc. Each of these steps should consist of a procedural test in a key area where the internal control has been judged satisfactory. A key area is one that has a significant effect on internal control. Tests of weak areas are not called for here, however, since these should already be covered in the weakness investigation.

The proposed supplementary tests can be recorded in terms of the "systems audit numbers" of the evidence to be checked. Again, for the same reasons as for the weakness investigation, these supplementary tests should be chosen during the systems audit but their execution should be deferred until the follow-up audit. An example is shown in Figure 8. (This shows the results, however, after the completion of the follow-up audit.) Since the tests are only supplementary confirmation of the auditor's initial evaluation, only a small portion of the total audit time should be devoted to this section. Except where internal control is almost ideal the auditor should expect to spend more time on the weakness investigation than on the supplementary tests. For external auditors, the extent of the supplementary tests may be reduced where reliance can be placed upon the testing procedures of the internal audit department. In repeat years the supplementary tests selected from each section should be different from those of the preceding one or two years. The aim should be over a period of three or four years to have these cyclical tests cover all key areas in those parts of the system judged to have satisfactory internal control.

"X" COMPANY LIMITED

CURRENT 19—1   *DH*   DEC. 19—1   SUPPLEMENTARY TESTS

Chart reference	Description of test	Initial	Results
B_2	Check that all credit notes are properly supported. (6-7-9) 200 (40 for 5 months)	*DH*	No errors found
C_1	Check that all accounts payable vouchers properly authorized and supported. (1-2-3) 250 (50 for 5 months)	*DH*	No errors found
D_3	Check accuracy of payroll distribution. (4-6-8) month of March complete	*DH*	No significant errors found
E_1	Check accuracy of burden absorption. (12-13) months of January and May	*DH*	No errors found

Figure 8. Supplementary tests.

Draft Memorandum of Recommendations

At the conclusion of the systems audit visit (the first stage of the analytical audit) the auditor can draft a memorandum of recommendations to the client covering all apparent weaknesses and inefficiencies noted on the outline charts.

Each recommendation should be drafted by the audit staff who reviewed the part of the system affected and it should be done *during*, not after, the systems audit visit. This makes maximum use of the systems knowledge acquired during the flow charting stage while it is still fresh. It is suggested, however, that the memorandum not be issued at this time but be held for more senior audit review between the visits and for further consideration during the follow-up audit.

A more senior review of the results of the systems audit visit will often suggest not only modifications in the proposed weakness investigation and supplementary tests (as described previously) but also changes in the recommendations to be made to the client. However, in many cases these changes must be rechecked with the client's employees to ensure that the recommendations, as they now stand, are really feasible. Failure to do this rechecking will often lead to suggestions which are impractical because of problems or obstacles which seem obvious to the client's employees but which the auditor has overlooked. One mistaken suggestion can detract from his advocacy of many worthwhile recommendations. The rechecking can conveniently be done during the follow-up audit. A second reason for deferring issue of a memorandum of recommendations is that it can then take into account any results of the follow-up audit which may be relevant. Occasionally a weakness will be obviously too costly to remove and no recommendation is therefore appropriate. (The weakness should still be noted on the outline charts, since it cannot be ignored from an audit point of view and must be included in the auditor's weakness investigation.)

In making recommendations on internal control several degrees of importance can be differentiated. First, some apparent weaknesses may be *so serious* that when a practical cure is available the auditor should concentrate his main efforts on persuading his client to adopt it. At the other extreme there are some weaknesses so minor that, though curable at little or no expense, their lesser importance must be clearly indicated so as not to detract from the critical points. A similar gradation in recommendations on efficiency can be seen. Again, it is only common sense to separate the important from the trivial in drafting the report. In addition, in making recommendations on efficiency the auditor should guard against exclusive concentration on procedural problems such as the flow and the processing of documents. These may often be minor in comparison to inadequacies in the employment of management accounting techniques, proper budgeting, and so on. Areas may also come to the auditor's notice where improvements should be considered, although they are to some extent outside the accounting field. There is no reason that, as a general practitioner who has completed a diagnostic review of the overall system, he should not point out areas which appear to deserve attention. For instance, his review of labour costing procedures may bring to his notice poor control over piecework labour or scope for incentives with respect to indirect labour. His review of inventory records may suggest the possibility of statistical scheduling.

In conjunction with his analysis of systems and procedures the auditor will also want to review income tax and sales tax points. Part of the auditor's regular annual service to his client should be advice on tax problems and tax planning. Many times this will indicate steps which should be taken without delay or, at least, taken during the current fiscal year. It may be too late to wait until the auditor is assessing the tax liabilities after the year-end. The systems audit is a useful time for the tax situation to be thoroughly reviewed. Any tax recommendations arising out of this review should therefore also be incorporated in the systems memorandum.

Oral Reporting of Points for Immediate Attention
Although in general the auditor's memorandum of recommendations will be more useful to his client if it is first carefully reviewed at the conclusion of the systems audit and rechecked during the follow-up audit, a few important exceptions must be noted. First, any serious errors discovered by the auditor must be reported immediately to the client (and recorded in the auditor's working papers). Secondly, the auditor may feel some major recommendations should be attended to immediately. These he will want to refer to the client right away, even if he subsequently reports on them at greater length in his memorandum. Finally, minor inefficiencies or systems weaknesses which the client might wish to attend to immediately may conveniently be taken up with him during the course of the audit. Simple improvements may often be more easily implemented through informal discussion with the client at the time. More involved suggestions, or those meeting some resistance, may better be left for the written memorandum.

Analytical Audit Report
Different practitioners prefer different methods of reporting and summarizing the results of field work. One example of an audit report used

in practice for summarizing the results of an analytical audit is set out in Appendix II. It is divided into two sections to correspond to the two stages of the audit: the systems audit and the follow-up audit. Space is provided for both the answers of the auditor who performed the field work and those of his superior who conducted the review.

Oral Review

Because of the concentration of information in analytical audit working papers a review of such a file encounters certain difficulties not present in the review of other types of working papers. A few comments on review methods for analytical auditing may therefore be of use. The best reviewing technique seems to be that of an *oral review* between audit senior and reviewer. The reviewer should *not* examine the analytical audit file prior to the oral review with the senior. Such an advance examination is likely to be time-consuming and less effective. It is more efficient for the reviewer, and a useful discipline for the senior, if the latter leads the reviewer through the file, explaining the system, and justifying his evaluation of the system by reference to the flow charts as he goes. The time spent on this review should not be excessive once some experience has been gained.

The oral review should be done as soon after the completion of the systems audit as possible and, best of all, at the client's office where additional information is available if needed. A suggested form for the oral review is as follows:

(a) The reviewer takes the first five minutes to read the description of the client's business (section A);

(b) For each section, starting with B and ending with F, the senior leads the reviewer briefly through:

    (i) The systems summary on the lead sheet;

    (ii) Each flow chart and related outline chart describing what the system is (a few details can be omitted),

    (iii) The apparent weaknesses and inefficiencies noted on the out-outline charts,

    (iv) Then, the primary internal control questions and his answers to them on the lead sheet.

(c) In reviewing the primary internal control questions on the lead sheet the senior should—

    (i) for each answer that the control was unsatisfactory, refer the reviewer to the indicated flow chart and to the weakness described on the related outline chart,

(ii) for each answer that the control was satisfactory, refer the reviewer to the indicated flow chart and demonstrate to him, on the flow chart, how the particular control is achieved.

(d) The senior should then refer the reviewer to the weakness follow-up sheet and explain how each proposed weakness investigation or balance sheet program revision is sufficient to detect any material errors that the apparent weakness might allow.

(e) Finally, the memorandum of recommendations, the supplementary tests, and the remaining sections in the file can be reviewed, ending with the analytical audit report itself.

The reviewer cannot expect to have the detailed knowledge of the system that the senior has, but he should, by a process of sceptical cross-examination throughout the above review, be able to establish whether or not the system has been properly evaluated and whether the proposed program for the follow-up visit is reasonable. During the review he should consider the following questions:

(a) Is the flow chart reasonably clear? Will next year's senior be able to read it?

(b) Is it too detailed or, conversely, not detailed enough?

(c) Does the flow chart support the senior's conclusions on the system evaluation?

(d) If a flow chart neither indicates an apparent weakness nor documents an internal control strength, was it really necessary?

(e) Is the apparent weakness more serious or less serious than the senior has concluded?

(f) Are the senior's answers indicating satisfactory control justified? Does the senior's justification make sense?

(g) Will the proposed weakness investigation or balance sheet program revision really detect material errors if they have occurred? Are the proposed steps too extensive or not extensive enough?

(h) Are the proposed supplementary tests reasonable (but not excessive) as an additional test confirmation of the senior's evaluation?

(i) Are the proposed recommendations to the client realistic? Do they really solve the problem? Has the proper priority been given according to relative importance? Have the recommendations been phrased intelligibly and persuasively?

(j) Have the other sections of the file been completed properly?

This review may well result in a number of changes to the internal control evaluation, the proposed follow-up audit, or the drafted recommendations. Or it may result in the senior being requested to obtain additional information on some point, rephrase certain recommendations, etc. Alternative recommendations raised during the review can, however, be investigated during the follow-up audit. After the oral review has been completed the reviewer may, if he feels it necessary, re-examine any sections of the file about which he is unsatisfied. Many times this will be unnecessary but, where it is, the rereading of certain working papers should take place *after,* and not before, the oral review with his senior.

Some Practical Advice

The foregoing completes the series of audit procedures comprising the systems audit. A few additional comments, about practical points to bear in mind during an actual engagement, may be useful.

PREPARATION

When an analytical audit is to be performed at an organization for the first time it is sometimes desirable to hold some preliminary discussion with the financial officers or accounting officers of that organization. This applies both to external and to internal auditors. Analytical auditing involves changes which will be readily apparent to the employees from whom the systems information will be obtained. It is as well to forestall questions. Anyone who expects the auditors to shut themselves up in the back room with "the books" and "get on with the audit" will be wondering what all the flow charting is about. A preliminary discussion might therefore review the general basis of the analytical auditing approach, its advantages, and certain changes the client may notice. A copy of the profile chart (Figure 2) may be a useful summary in explaining the approach briefly.

In scheduling the work of an analytical audit for the first time the auditor should bear a number of factors in mind. The systems audit can be done early in the year. Flow charting, of course, will be difficult during the client's peak period or, conversely, when many employees are on vacation. A small audit staff (one to three persons) is more efficient than a large staff. While very junior staff can be used for certain portions of *repeat year* audits they are best avoided in *first year* analytical audits. (Investing the time of experienced staff in the first year during the initial preparation of the flow charts will pay dividends in the repeat year audits.) Some preliminary time must be spent on completing the description of the business (section A), on preparing a time budget by section, and on planning the assignment of flow charting sections before any charting should be started. This preliminary work is essential if the systems audit is to be conducted efficiently.

WORK ASSIGNMENT

On a small engagement one auditor may be doing the whole job himself, in which case it is usually best, though not essential, to work through the sections in the order B to F. On a larger engagement the auditor will be assigning some sections to his assistants. The whole of any given section (that is, all the flow charts, the lead sheet and the evaluation) should be done by one person. It is inefficient to have several people working on related flow charts in the section: many of the interrelationships may be missed and the overall design of the section may be piecemeal and disorganized.

In assigning sections to his staff the senior might remember that, for a first year audit: (1) purchasing and payables (section C) is usually the most straightforward and hence should be assigned to his most junior assistant; (2) payrolls (section D) is not too complicated as a rule and can be assigned to reasonably junior staff; (3) sales (section B) is often one of the hardest to chart in the first year (because of the number of alternatives to be covered) and so should be assigned to an experienced staff member; (4) the cost system (section E), because of its complexity, is difficult to chart, at least for a manufacturer, and should therefore be done by the auditor himself or by his most experienced assistant; (5) section F (on books of account and monthly statements) is best done *after* the other sections are completed and should usually be done by the auditor himself; (6) there will be many exceptions to the above rules in practice but these will be recognized by the auditor who has done his preliminary field work before his assistants arrive. In repeat years the above points will be less critical, though still significant.

TIME SUMMARY AND BUDGET

Auditors are familiar with the advantages of preparing a time summary of the current year's work and a time budget for the next year. In the analytical auditing approach it is desirable that the time analysis be taken to the point of showing time for each systems section and *for each individual flow chart*. At first glance this may seem needlessly detailed. But a moment's reflection will show that the detail can lead to large time savings. The importance of budgeting by individual flow chart is that the time specified for a given chart helps to tell the audit staff the degree of detail and thoroughness which is expected on that part of the systems audit. Important control areas deserve intensive review and the time for such a chart may be several times greater than the time appropriate for a less important chart. In other words, the audit staff should be guided not so much by the complexity of a given part of the system, but more by its *relative importance,* in deciding the systems audit time appropriate for it. The time budget figures by flow chart serve, in part, as a job description for the charter and should be assigned accordingly when setting the proposed budget for the next year.

Of course, the auditor on a first-year analytical audit must remember that the following year's systems audit time, when the flow charts have only to be up-dated, should be much less than (probably about one half) the first-year systems audit time. A convenient plan is to set the next year's time budget by flow chart on the basis that no extensive recharting for major systems changes will be required (unless such changes are already known to be planned). Then there can be included in the total time budget a reasonable allowance for work on charting systems changes (but unallocated to specific charts since the auditor cannot predict where the revisions will arise).

RETENTION OF WORKING PAPERS

For the sake of efficiency the flow charts in an analytical audit file should generally be prepared in pencil so that they may be carried forward and revised where necessary with a minimum of difficulty in future years. The flow charts, however, contain both the record of the systems audit performed by the auditor and an important part of the record of his evaluation of control. If these charts are carried forward and revised in future years the question arises as to what record is left behind to document the auditor's work for past years. (This point will be more important for external auditors than for internal auditors.)

One solution to this problem is to prepare brief extracts of the systems audit program to be retained as a permanent record. Extracts have the disadvantage of duplicating some of the audit documentation already summarized more accurately and more efficiently on the flow charts themselves. A better solution is to retain photocopies of the key flow charts (thus documenting both the systems and the systems audit of past years). Finally, a convenient alternative to retaining photocopies is to microfilm key flow charts at the conclusion of the audit. The charts themselves are then free to be re-used or revised in future years, while a record is still preserved of the auditor's systems review and systems audit in the past. There is no problem, of course, in retaining a record of the follow-up audit since it will be desirable to prepare a new weakness follow-up sheet each year anyway.

CHAPTER

6

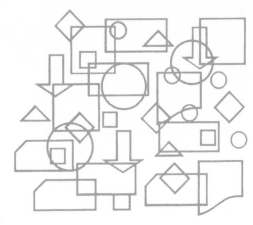

THE FOLLOW-UP AUDIT

In Chapter 5 the components of the first stage (the systems audit) were discussed at length. The present chapter reviews the steps to be performed in completing the second stage (the follow-up audit). Less need be said about this second stage since the drafting of the weakness investigation itself has already been discussed in describing the systems audit.

Statistics Analysis

Before completing the programs of weakness investigation and supplementary tests which were drafted during the systems audit, it is useful for the auditor to do some checking of the self-consistency of financial figures, ratios, trends, and other statistics pertaining to the client's operations. It is true that analyses and comparisons of various profit and loss components are traditionally included in the auditor's work following the year-end. These are still needed. But the analytical audit is a convenient time to conduct a more fundamental analysis of the statistics available before the annual rush to meet audit deadlines. The nature of and amount of emphasis to be placed on this statistics analysis will vary from audit to audit and no precise rules can be given. The purpose is (a) to gain assurance as to the accuracy of the accounting system through the reasonableness and consistency of the various statistics, reports, comparisons, budgets, analyses, etc. which most businesses produce and (b) to locate in these reports and statistics any unusual or unexpected relationships which would warrant additional audit investigation. This might be called a "businessman's approach to auditing." Frequently, statistics analysis will provide the auditor with important information faster than an examination of large samples of documents.

The reason for leaving the statistics analysis until the second stage of the analytical audit is so that the major portion of the year's results will be available for consideration. The reason for making this analysis before completing the weakness investigation, however, is so that any apparent anomalies in the statistics can be used as a basis for revising or extending the audit investigation where appropriate. While the design of this section of the audit is very much up to the initiative of the auditor, a number of suggestions can be given. The analysis must, of course, be limited to what it is possible to do in a reasonable time. Some calculations might be simple to make on one engagement and almost impossible on another. The following suggestions, therefore, are neither invariable nor necessarily complete.

Receivable levels can be compared to credit terms. That is, the number of days of *preceding* sales on hand in any month-end total of receivables should be reasonably related to the credit terms and to a knowledge of the proportion of customers taking discounts (which can be computed from the figure for cash discounts expense). Inventory levels can be compared to purchase lead times, production cycles and finished-goods stocking policies. For instance, the number of days of *succeeding* materials consumption on hand in any month-end total of raw materials should be reasonably related to the average lead times used in purchasing. The number of days *succeeding* cost of goods completed on hand in any month-end total of work in process should be reasonably related to the average production cycle multiplied by average state of completion. The number of days of *succeeding* cost of sales on hand in any month-end total of finished goods should be reasonably related to finished-goods stocking policies. Monthly gross profit (in total or by product line) can be compared to the average gross profit of a sample of shipments. Reported labour costs can be compared with average wage rate times number of employees. If a standard cost system is used, all significant variances should be analyzed and explained. If any totals of physical units of production or sales are available (e.g. number of articles, tons, barrels, gallons, etc.), they may be multiplied by average cost or selling price and compared to reported cost of production or reported sales. All significant deviations from budget should be analyzed and explained. Any unusual trends (such as sales commissions increasing during a period of falling sales, etc.) should be questioned. Finally, any other contradictory or inconsistent figures noted in the review of the monthly statements, or management exception reports or in the scrutiny of the accounting records should be investigated.

In all the above steps the auditor should try to check the consistency of one figure with another (e.g. receivables, sales and credit terms) or of one figure with known facts (e.g. labour costs with number of employees) rather than merely comparing the same figure for two different periods (e.g. labour costs this month with labour costs last month). Checking the comparability with prior periods is a useful step but not enough by itself, since a similar shortage or discrepancy might easily exist throughout all these periods.

On some engagements the statistics analysis in total will take only a small amount of time. On others, the analysis—especially the analysis of deviations from budget—may justify a large portion of the total audit time. The auditor must, of course, prepare a proper summary of the analysis, comparisons, and calculations done and the conclusions drawn. Occasionally, some inconsistency or anomaly may be encountered for which no satisfactory explanation is forthcoming. Some additional audit investigation (as opposed to mere comparisons and calculations) may be required to resolve the question. In these cases, the problem and the planned investigation should be incorporated in the weakness investigation and recorded on the weakness follow-up sheet. For instance, an unfavourable and unexplained labour quantity variance may suggest poor control over direct labour and call for some investigation to see if any significant "over-booking" of piece work is occurring. In a sense the unexplained variance, until resolved, is an apparent weakness just as much as is a weakness observed in the structure of the system on the flow charts.

Weakness Investigation

The weakness investigation as drafted during the systems audit and as reviewed can now be performed. It should include any additional work necessary to cover unresolved statistical discrepancies (as discussed above). The results should then be summarized on the weakness follow-up sheet (Figure 7). Where errors are encountered in doing the weakness investigation, it may be necessary to extend the scope of the work to resolve the matter one way or the other. It should be remembered, however, that the purpose is to establish whether or not a material amount of error has occurred over the year. Immaterial errors may not matter in themselves unless their frequency in the investigational work raises the possibility of a material total of such errors over the year. The results found in the weakness investigation may also necessitate changing the proposed revisions in the balance sheet audit program.

Supplementary Tests

The supplementary tests as drafted during the systems audit and as reviewed can now be performed. The results should be summarized appropriately (Figure 8). If any errors are encountered they should be recorded in the working papers and the evaluation of internal control *reconsidered*. These tests are being done in areas where the internal control was judged to be satisfactory. Errors therefore mean that a mistaken conclusion was drawn and some part of the system is not functioning in the way previously thought. This in turn could indicate a weakness more far-reaching than the particular errors just encountered. Therefore, if errors are found (using reasonable judgment as to what constitutes a significant "error" for this purpose) the auditor *should not extend* the supplementary test but reconsider the evaluation of internal control. If this in turn indicates a weakness, he should record it on the appropriate outline chart and include appropriate procedures in the weakness investigation (or balance sheet program revision) to cover the risk of *material* errors arising from the weakness.

Enquiry About Systems Changes

The auditor should enquire from officials of the organization whether personnel or systems changes that would affect the internal control have occurred since the time of the systems audit visit. This enquiry should not, of course, have the scope of a full-fledged systems audit again because it is impractical to attempt to verify the system in force at every instant throughout the year. The enquiry should, however, be sufficient to determine whether any significant element of internal control, present at the time of the systems audit, has since disappeared. If so, an appropriate weakness investigation should be devised and carried out. While any decrease in internal control should be covered by appropriate weakness investigation, no apparent increase in internal control should be relied upon. This is because the new system in force will not be fully verified until the next year's systems audit. (These points are of less concern to the internal auditor, for he can likely keep more up to date in his flow charts and in his systems reviews than is feasible for the external auditor.)

Informal Discussion of Recommendations

When the follow-up audit has been completed, the auditor can discuss the comments and suggestions made in the draft memorandum with the employees who might be affected thereby (using reasonable discretion). The purpose is to ensure that the suggestions are realistic and workable before the auditor formally presents them to his client. If a new procedure is being proposed the auditor should make sure it can really be implemented without raising other problems. If the elimination of some old procedure is being proposed he must make sure that all effects of its elimination have been considered and any problems solved. All discussions should be tentative and informal at this point—and not at too senior a level. The aim is not to review the memorandum as such but to discuss the possibilities for the changes it proposes. Using reasonable discretion means, of course, (a) avoiding undue criticism of the present system or of present employees, and (b) refraining from gratuitous explanations to the employees involved of how a given weakness could be exploited. The discussions may indicate a number of obstacles or objections to proposed changes in the draft memorandum. The auditor may agree with some of these objections, in which case he should amend the draft memorandum accordingly. Others he may feel are invalid. In these cases it may be useful to answer the objections in advance in the memorandum and explain how the apparent difficulties can be overcome.

Oral Review

An oral review can be done upon the completion of the follow-up audit. This oral review will normally be quite short (much more so than that following the systems audit visit). It is limited to: (a) reviewing the design and results of the statistics analysis; (b) reviewing the results of the weakness investigation and supplementary tests and considering whether any additional action taken by the senior, as a result of errors found, has been adequate; (c) discussing any modifications made since the original, approved draft of the memorandum of recommendations. Following this, the memorandum of recommendations can be issued to the client. As the issuing of audited financial statements marks the end of the normal balance sheet audit, so the issuing of a letter of recommendations marks the end of the 'normal analytical audit.

Some Practical Advice

PLANNING

In scheduling the follow-up visit it should be remembered that the follow-up audit can usually be done late in the year so that as many as possible of the year's results are available to audit. Normally this visit involves far less time than the systems audit. The late scheduling does not therefore create serious peak problems. On the other hand, the longer the follow-up visit occurs after the systems audit, the less detailed familiarity with the system can the auditor retain. On some analytical audits the statistics analysis (see below) may assume major proportions and so should not be left too late in the year. Hence, some compromise between these different factors is necessary. For clients at locations some distance from the auditor it may be impractical to make two analytical audit visits; the systems audit and follow-up audit may have to be done on the same visit. In these cases, it is desirable that the working papers from the systems audit be reviewed on location, before the follow-up audit is commenced.

WORK ASSIGNMENT

The weakness investigation and the supplementary tests can be assigned to junior audit staff provided they are adequately supervised. The statistics analysis is best left, however, for more senior audit staff to perform. Senior audit staff should also be used to bring up to date the scrutiny of appropriate books and records begun in the systems audit.

CHAPTER

7

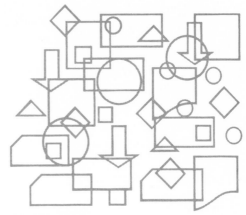

EXAMPLES OF SYSTEMS SECTIONS

Chapters 5 and 6 have described analytical auditing procedures in some detail. The general procedures outlined are the same whether the auditor is working on the sales-receivables-receipts section, the purchases-payables-payments section, or the payroll section. However, there is naturally some variation in the problems which are peculiar to each of these different sections. In the present chapter each of these sections of a total system will be examined, its contents discussed, and examples of its flow charts given. It is impossible, of course, to give examples of flow charts for every different type of business and system that can be encountered in practice. Those illustrated in this chapter are only a few of the many possible types. They are not intended to represent particularly good, bad or even "average" systems. All of the charts illustrated happen to be for a small manufacturing company. But this does not mean that flow charting cannot apply equally well to wholesalers, retailers, insurance companies, banks, mines, oil and gas companies, publishing companies, stockbrokers, utilities, construction companies, etc. A manufacturing business merely serves as a useful general example of the expenditure of material and labour to produce goods or services for sale. Most industries involve these same activities and it is only their form that varies.

Sales-Receivables-Receipts

The components of this section would normally include (though not necessarily in this order):

(1) a method of selling price determination (price lists or individual quotes or tenders)

(2) the receipt of a customer's order (by mail, phone, salesman, etc.)

(3) the preparation, usually, of some standard internal order

   (4) recording of the order (in a register or by filing, etc.)
   (5) any necessary editing, coding, numbering, quoting, approving, classifying, taking of control totals, etc.
   (6) some system of credit approval
   (7) up-dating of inventory control and/or production scheduling records
   (8) requisitioning from stock or initiating of necessary purchase or production orders
   (9) the preparation of various shipping orders, bills of lading, back orders, etc.
 (10) the preparation of sales invoices
 (11) the pricing of sales invoices and checking of such prices
 (12) the calculating of sales tax, freight, delivery charges, trade discounts, cash discounts, volume rebates, etc.
 (13) the recording and summarizing of the sale in a sales journal, summary or listing
 (14) the costing of such sale (sometimes)
 (15) the posting and trial balancing of accounts receivable records and preparation of customers' statements
 (16) the handling, recording, balancing, depositing, posting and summarizing of cash receipts
 (17) the treatment of credit notes, returned goods, price adjustments, invoice errors, write-offs, etc.
 (18) the procedures of credit control and collection
 (19) the preparation of various sales statistics
 (20) the recording of cash sales, C.O.D. sales, employee sales, fixed asset sales, scrap sales, consignments, direct shipments from supplier to customer, etc.
 (21) the coordination with outward freight procedures
 (22) the recording and control of miscellaneous cash receipts.

Basically, the system begins with data received from some customer and ends with the conversion of some material, service or inventory into an account receivable, and ultimately into cash. The accounting entries involved are some form of sales entry and some form of cash receipts entry. Entries can be complicated by partial orders, progress billings, payments on account, accounts receivable adjustments, and so on. The sales order, shipping order, and sales invoice may be three separate documents or all copies of one combined order-invoice. Orders may be controlled right from the point of receipt (to guard against unfilled orders) or merely from the point of shipment (to guard against unbilled shipments).

Not all of the above points will be equally important in every system. In any case, some have more bearing on internal control, and hence are of more concern to the auditor, than others. For instance, unfilled orders do not distort the financial statements but unbilled shipments do. Inaccurate sales statistics may hinder proper sales forecasting, but pricing errors or posting mistakes affect the reliability of the reported results. All of these may be a source of useful suggestions to the client (secondary objective), but only those affecting the accounting reliability will influence the external auditor's opinion (primary objective). Hence, the degree of completeness and detail of the flow charting in these areas should be set accordingly. (For the internal auditor the relative emphasis may be different.)

Charting of Sales-Receivables-Receipts

In rare cases it may be possible to combine this whole section on one flow chart. Usually, however, it must be divided into two or more charts such as (a) sales and receivables and (b) cash receipts, or (a) sales (b) receivables (c) cash receipts (d) credit notes, and so on. A common problem is the number of different types of sales encountered—each with a different method of processing. This calls for judgment in selecting the best way of showing the alternatives.

A sales chart and related outline chart have already been illustrated in Figures 4 and 5 and discussed in Chapter 4. It will be recalled that this chart covered orders, shipments, billing and accounting, but did not cover cash sales, cash receipts or credit note preparation. In this case these would be covered on separate flow charts. For instance, the related flow chart for cash sales and cash receipts is illustrated in Figure 9 and the corresponding outline chart in Figure 10.

It may be useful to see how the basic questions on internal control (per Appendix III) are answered by these flow charts. Can goods be shipped but not invoiced? It can be seen on Figure 4 that the billing clerk has no way of knowing that she receives every SO_2 from shipping (since she files them alphabetically). Accordingly, she cannot be sure that she has prepared an invoice for every shipment. Nor is there any other place in the system where copies of the invoices are matched to complete files of shipping orders (or marked off in the order register) to ensure that there is an invoice for every order. This weakness has therefore been noted on the outline chart (Figure 5).

Can goods be shipped to a bad credit risk? Any credit approval would have to appear somewhere in the first two columns in Figure 4. No such approval is there. Of course, the auditor does not wait until his flow chart is complete to ask such questions. He must be thinking of these control questions all the time he is conducting his systems review. In his discussion

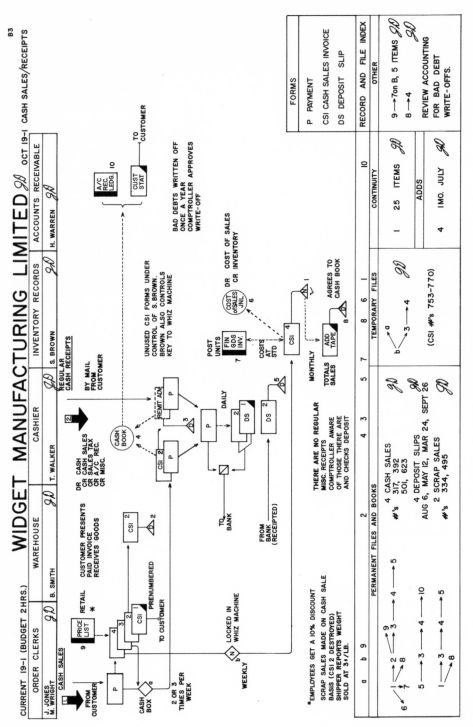

Figure 9. Flow chart of cash sales and cash receipts.

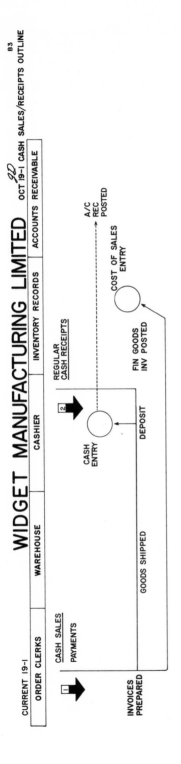

Figure 10. Outline chart of cash sales and cash receipts.

with the order clerks he will certainly raise the point when he notices that the systems information they have just given him does not include any credit approval (they may merely have forgotten to tell him). In this example, the order clerks have replied that there is no formal approval but that they know the bad accounts fairly well. It is doubtful whether such a system can be very safe since the order clerks are not likely to know the current receivable level and collection status of each account. This weakness has therefore been noted on the outline chart (Figure 5) as well.

Can sales be invoiced but not recorded in the accounts? With respect to credit sales the flow chart (Figure 4) shows that once a prenumbered invoice has been issued the system provides reasonable assurance that it is properly accounted for. The mechanics of this particular control were discussed on page 59. However, with respect to cash sales the flow chart (Figure 9) shows a significant weakness, in that cash sales proceeds are held by a clerk who enters both the sales journal and the cash book. He therefore would be in a position to misappropriate cash sales proceeds and conceal the shortage by omitting identical amounts from the entries in the sales journal and the additions in the cash book (accounts receivable would remain in balance). The fact that he is in a position to steal does not, of course, make him a thief. He may be the most honest employee in the world. But the system itself does not provide any assurance on this point and the internal control cannot therefore be said to be adequate. This weakness is noted on the outline chart (Figure 10). It will be assumed, in this example, that the cash sales part of the business is substantial and therefore this weakness is of some significance.

Can receivables be credited improperly? The answer to this question depends upon the procedures for initiating and processing credit notes and bad debt write-offs. The flow chart covering the credit note procedures is not illustrated in this chapter so the question cannot be dealt with here.

Is lapping possible? The only person who handles customers' remittances is the cashier, T. Walker. There is no question that he could misappropriate cash and cover up any shortage in a customer's account by lapping. He can theoretically record any name he wants in the cash book and the amount will be credited to that customer by H. Warren. However, Walker has no control over customer statements, follow-up of overdue accounts, or customer queries. A lapping operation would therefore be very dangerous and subject to exposure at any time. This is certainly not a guaranteed protection against lapping but the control can probably be considered to be reasonable. In any case, what slight risk there is pales in comparison to the obvious danger of misappropriated cash sales (already discussed above).

Can payments be received and not deposited? This question has already been answered in discussing the danger of misappropriated cash sales. (Sometimes control questions will be found to overlap in this way—particularly where control is weak).

Can overdue accounts escape attention? The control over overdue accounts rests solely with the accounts receivable posting clerk, H. Warren. Some more senior review would be desirable. Figure 4 shows that Warren does send an aged trial balance to the comptroller every month, but the comptroller does nothing with it apart from agreeing the total to the monthly financial statements. Exactly what the comptroller does with the trial balance may not be entirely explicit on the flow chart. Nor does the flow chart show whether H. Warren has sufficient experience and ability as a credit manager that no more senior review is necessary. Both these points, however, will be assesssed by the auditor who is thinking in terms of control while he conducts his review and prepares his flow charts. The weakness noted on the outline chart (Figure 5) would indicate that the auditor has decided the review of overdue accounts is inadequate.

Can sales be invoiced but not costed? The flow chart (Figure 4) shows that numerical control is kept of sales invoices after the point at which they are entered in the cost of sales journal. While this control is not absolutely foolproof (an invoice could be filed but not entered) the system can probably be considered reasonable under the circumstances.

Can invoicing errors occur? Both for credit sales (Figure 4) and for cash sales (Figure 9) there is no second check or test check of invoice pricing. Both these weaknesses are noted on the outline charts (Figures 5 and 10), although for cash sales the absence of a second check is normal and the magnitude of potential error probably not too great.

Purchases-Payables-Payments

The components of this section would normally include (though not necessarily in this order):

(1) a method of determining when materials are to be ordered (material forecasts or automatic re-order points or specific orders for sales contracts, etc.)

(2) the preparation of purchase requisitions (sometimes)

(3) the preparation and approval of purchase orders (usually)

(4) the receipt of goods and recording of quantities (and check of quantities) received (complete orders and partial orders)

(5) the preparation of receiving slips or inspection reports, etc.

(6) the receipt of the supplier's invoice

(7) the matching, checking (comparisons, additions, extensions, sales tax, etc.) and recording of the invoice, receiving slip, and purchase order

(8) the entering of the account distribution (on invoices or purchase orders)

(9) the preparation of a cheque and (sometimes) voucher jacket covering a group of invoices

(10) approvals, initials, signatures and countersignatures of invoices, vouchers, and cheques

(11) the recording of vouchers payable and cheques issued in voucher register, or purchase journal or cheque register (and posting to accounts payable ledger where one is used)

(12) the balancing of accounts payable to general ledger control

(13) the recording of the distribution of costs by inventory sub-account and expense classification

(14) the reconciling of bank accounts, processing of cancelled cheques and bank statements, etc.

(15) the reconciling of creditors' statements

(16) the issuing of debit notes for short shipments, price adjustments, invoicing errors, etc. and reconciling with credit notes received

(17) up-dating of inventory records (posting)

(18) the recording of fixed asset purchases, consignments, direct shipments from supplier to customer, etc., miscellaneous disbursements, petty cash expenditures

(19) the special treatment of invoices offering cash discounts for early payment

(20) the coordination with inward freight procedures; freight payments

(21) the computation of variances on purchase prices (where a standard cost system used) or calculation of FIFO or average cost, etc.

Basically, the system begins with a materials requirement, as determined internally, proceeds with the issue of orders, and ends with the conversion of cash into an inventory cost or expense. The accounting entries involved are some form of purchase entry and some form of cash disbursements entry (the two may be combined). The purchase order and receiving report may be separate documents or copies of the same form. Travelling purchase requisitions may be employed which permit re-use. Again, not all of the above points will be of equal concern to the auditor. For instance, purchasing unneeded goods may lead to overstocking but does not distort the accounts. Incorrect distributions or improper payments, on the other hand, directly affect the accuracy of the reported results. Again, the degree of detail of the flow charting must be selected according to the relative importance of each area as it affects the audit opinion.

In rare cases it may be possible to combine this whole system on one flow chart. Usually, however, the system must be divided into at least two charts: (a) accounts payable disbursements involving purchase orders, and (b) miscellaneous disbursements involving no purchase orders. For a larger system there may also have to be separate charts for (c) fixed asset purchases, (d) freight procedures, and so on. In general, purchases-payables-payments will be the easiest section in the file to chart.

Figure 11 shows an example of a purchase flow chart for a small manufacturing company. Payables and payments would, in this case, be covered on a separate chart. Review of this chart will show one apparent weakness in control, in that suppliers' invoices are routed through the purchasing department rather than being sent directly to accounts payable. A couple of inefficiencies are also evident. File d would be better kept in alphabetical order—which would facilitate matching with the suppliers' invoices. The processing of the second invoice copy could probably be eliminated if the standard cost were recorded on the purchase order so that the accounts payable clerk could compute the price variance. The systems audit at the bottom of the chart flows in a grave-to-cradle direction (as is normal for this section) beginning with a file of paid invoices (I and PO₃), shown as file 2 on the next flow chart (C₂). The systems audit on the payments chart (C₂) would, of course, begin with the cancelled cheque itself.

Payrolls

The components of this section would normally include (though not necessarily in this order):

(1) the hiring of employees, creation of personnel records, rate authorizations, etc.
(2) the termination of employees
(3) the treatment of rate changes
(4) the control of time through clock cards, work tickets, etc.
(5) the receipt of time or piece work records for payroll processing
(6) the preparation of intermediate listings, summaries, clock card and work ticket reconciliations
(7) the preparation of the gross payroll and net payroll
(8) procedures for payroll deductions
(9) the preparation of payroll cheques or cash pay envelopes, method of signing, etc.
(10) the method of pay distribution
(11) procedures for unclaimed wages, vacations, advances, pay-offs, etc.
(12) the preparation of employees' earnings records

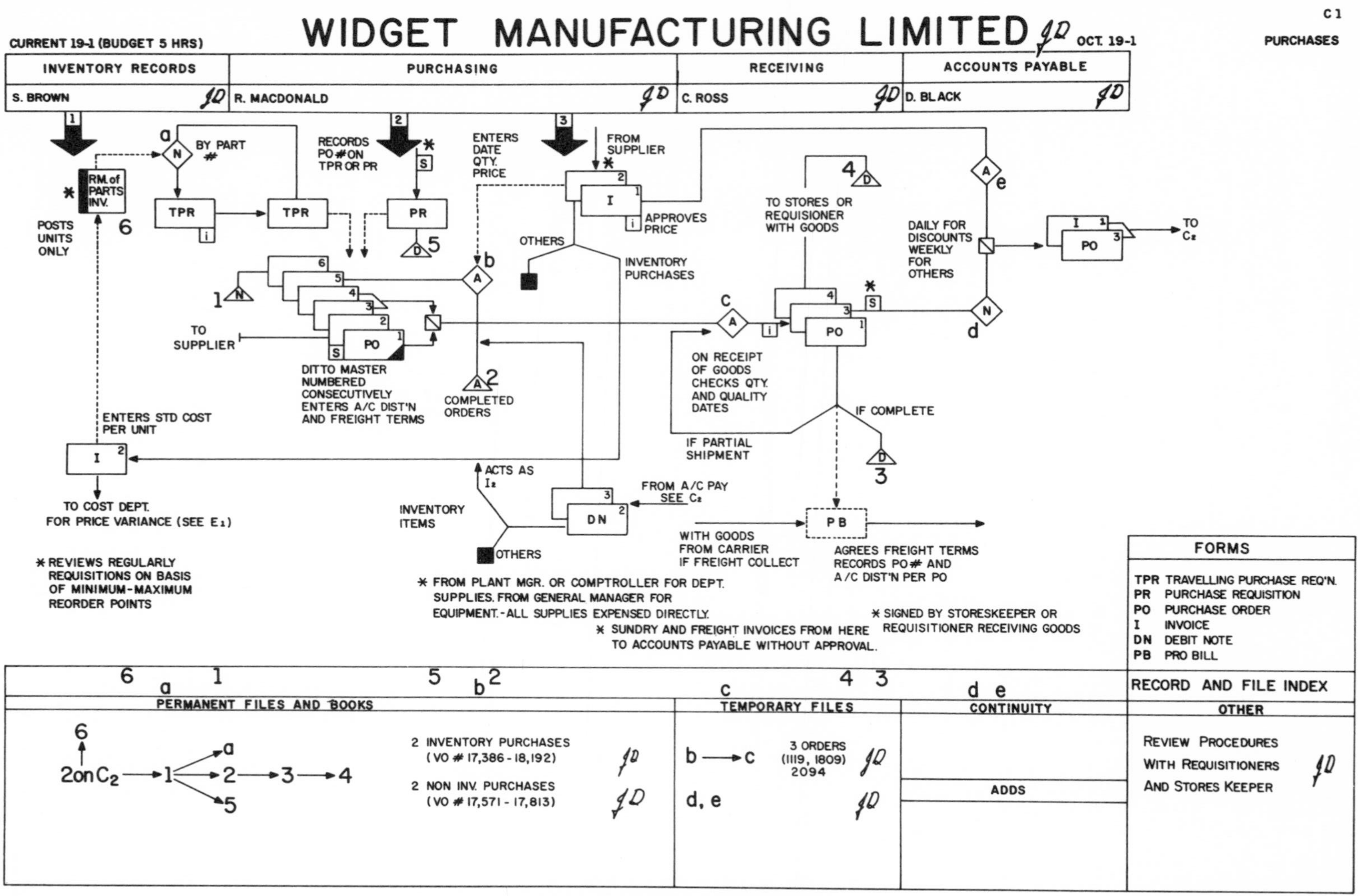

Figure 11. Flow chart of purchases.

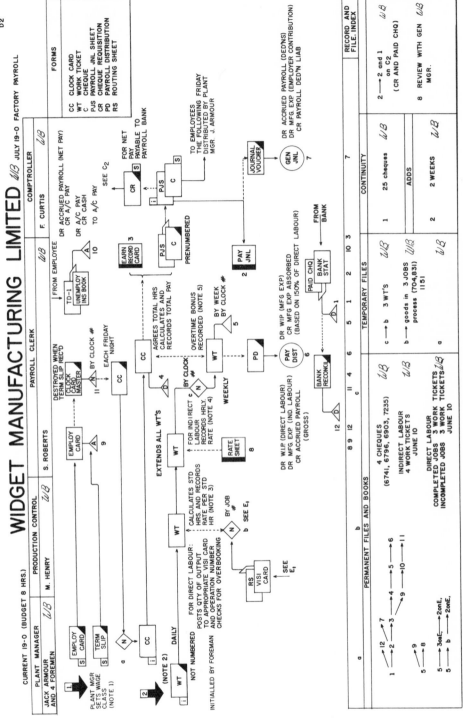

Figure 12. Flow chart of factory payroll.

(13) the reconciliation of payroll changes to hiring, termination, and rate change information

(14) a system of payroll approvals

(15) reconciliation of piece-work quantities to production data

(16) calculations of incentives, bonuses, overtime, part-time, etc.

(17) the preparation of the payroll distribution charging wages and salaries to inventory sub-accounts and expense accounts

(18) up-dating of inventory records (posting)

(19) the reconciliation of payroll bank accounts

(20) use of direct labour and indirect labour costs and hours to compute overhead absorption rates, etc.

(21) use of direct labour cost or hours to absorb present overhead.

Basically, the system begins with labour information being received from the office, field, or plant and ends with the conversion of cash into an inventory cost or expense. The accounting entries involved are some form of payroll payment entry and some form of payroll cost distribution entry. Again, not all of the above points will be of equal concern to the auditor. For instance, the hiring of poor factory workers may inhibit production but does not affect accounting reliability. On the other hand, errors in the distribution of labour charges may affect the accuracy of the inventory valuation. Again, the degree of detail of the different flow charts must be chosen accordingly.

In most cases this section can be divided into two charts: (1) plant wages and (2) office salaries. In some cases the charts may have to be further divided into (a) the hiring and firing of employees and (b) the preparation of the required daily, weekly, or monthly payroll. Figure 12 shows an example of the factory payroll chart for a small manufacturing company. The system involves work tickets, clock cards, and payments by cheque. Notes 1 to 5 refer to brief additional explanatory notes on a following page (which is not reproduced here). Weaknesses to be noticed on the chart are that the payroll calculations are not checked, bank reconciliation is not segregated from payroll preparation, and the same employee is responsible both for hiring and for distributing the pay.

Cost Section

The foregoing pages have reviewed the contents and charting of sales-receivables-receipts (section B), purchases-payables-payments (section C), and payrolls (section D). The remaining sections: cost and inventory records (section E) and books of account and monthly financial statements (section F) involve certain differences from the previous three. These are discussed below.

Almost every enterprise that sells goods or services has some form of cost system. But not every such system will require a cost section in the analytical audit file. If cost of sales is determined merely on the basis of a year-end inventory count, the "cost system" is so rudimentary that no separate section is necessary to review it. Or, consider the case of a distributor who uses a FIFO cost system for costing sales and valuing inventories. The unit costs are probably calculated and recorded as an integral part of the purchasing system (section C). The costing of sales is probably a regular part of the sales procedures (section B). The posting of inventory records would be dealt with in both sections. No separate cost section (section E) is therefore required for this cost system. On the other hand, in the case of a manufacturer, neither the sales nor purchasing sections would touch on the subject of, say, material consumption. A separate cost section (section E) would therefore be necessary.

The plan should be that all aspects of costing that are handled as part of regular procedures in other sections are charted in those other sections. The remainder of the costing function should then be covered in the cost section. In general, for a manufacturing firm: (a) cost of sales and the relieving of finished goods inventory records is handled in the sales section; (b) purchasing of materials and supplies for production and the posting of raw material inventory records is handled in the purchasing section; (c) charging of labour to overhead and to work in process is handled in the payroll section (and possibly the absorption of overhead as well, if based on labour); and (d) depreciation charged to overhead is handled in the books of account section.

Thus, the cost section (section E) is left to include:

(1) any of the above functions (a) to (d) which cannot be conveniently charted in the sections indicated

(2) material and supplies consumption (transfer of raw materials to work in process and supplies to overhead)

(3) production and scrap (transfer of work in process to finished goods or scrap)

(4) absorption of overhead (transfer of overhead to work in process) where it is not a part of the regular payroll procedures

(5) any other cost functions which are not a regular part of the other sections, such as: preparation and revision of standards; job costing (where it is handled outside the regular sales, purchasing and payroll systems); and determination of variances not covered elsewhere

(6) a summary of cost entries—so that the overall design of the cost accounting can be seen in one place (even though many of the entries themselves will originate in other sections).

In the simplest case items (1) to (5) above can be recorded on a normal flow chart covering the flow of records and documents and their summarization; item (6) can be set out on a separate schedule of skeleton cost entries. In more complicated cases the charting of items (1) to (5) must be spread over several cost flow charts.

The easiest place to start may be with the skeleton cost entries. One particular example for a small manufacturing company is set out in Figure 13. Here the first three entries and the last entry relate to procedures already charted in other sections (purchases, payrolls and sales) while the remaining four entries relate to procedures which must now be charted on the cost flow chart. The flow of information producing these four entries can be most easily seen by turning now to the outline chart (Figure 14). Once this outline is clear to the reader he can refer to the related flow chart (Figure 15). Cost systems by their nature are often more complicated than other parts of the accounting system; the flow charting of the cost section therefore calls for more careful organization and for greater experience than do the other sections. In the particular system illustrated it will be seen that cost entries can easily be missed if various documents from the factory go astray before reaching the cost department; also there is no control to ensure that recorded production is represented by measured additions to finished goods. These weaknesses are noted on the outline chart (Figure 14).

Books of Account

The previous four sections in the analytical audit file take the processing up to the point of posting sources to the general ledger. In the books of account section (section F) an organization type chart can be used to show the gathering of the various books of account together into the general ledger. An example is shown in Figure 16. A different type of audit strip can be used at the bottom of this chart to cover scrutiny for the year, posting for one month, trial balancing the general ledger, adding the general ledger, and clearing the opening entries in the general ledger. For a small organization a complete check (e.g. complete posting for one month) takes little time to perform. For a large organization, however, many of the audit steps should be done on a test basis.

WIDGET MANUFACTURING LIMITED

CURRENT 19-1 (BUDGET 1 HOUR) *CM* OCT. 19-1 COST ENTRIES E_2

ENTRY	SUB-ACCOUNTS	BASIS	REFERENCE
PURCHASES DR MANUFACTURING EXPENSE DR RAW MATERIAL AND PARTS INVENTORY CR ACCOUNTS PAYABLE	BY 4 DEPTS. EACH 30 a/c's	AT ACTUAL COST AT ACTUAL COST-SUBSEQUENTLY ADJUSTED TO STANDARD -SEE PRICE VARIANCE ENTRY BELOW	C_2
PAYROLL DR W.I.P. (DIRECT LABOUR) DR MANUFACTURING EXPENSE (INDIRECT LABOUR) CR ACCRUED PAYROLL	BY 4 DEPTS. EACH 5 a/c's	AT ACTUAL, BUT DIRECT LABOUR IS AN INCENTIVE SYSTEM USING STANDARD HOURS. ∴ DIRECT LABOUR IS AT STANDARD	D_2
DR W.I.P. (MANUFACTURING EXPENSE) CR MANUFACTURING EXPENSE ABSORBED		150% OF DIRECT LABOUR	D_2
MATERIALS CONSUMPTION DR W.I.P. (MATERIALS AND PARTS) DR or CR MANUFACTURING EXPENSE (MATERIALS USAGE VARIANCE) CR RAW MATERIAL AND PARTS INVENTORY		AT STANDARD COST AT STANDARD COST OF EXCESS REQUISITIONS	E_1
PRODUCTION DR FINISHED GOODS INVENTORY CR W.I.P. (MATERIAL, LABOUR, MANUFACTURING EXPENSE)		AT STANDARD COST	E_1
SCRAP DR MANUFACTURING EXPENSE (PRODUCTION SCRAP) CR W.I.P. (MATERIAL, LABOUR, MANUFACTURING EXPENSE)	BY 4 DEPTS.	AT STANDARD COST	E_1
PRICE VARIANCE DR or CR MATERIALS PRICE VARIANCE CR or DR RAW MATERIAL AND PARTS INVENTORY		TO ADJUST ACTUAL TO STANDARD	E_1
COST OF SALES DR COST OF SALES CR FINISHED GOODS INVENTORY	BY 8 SALES CATEGORIES	AT STANDARD	B_2

Figure 13. Skeleton cost entries.

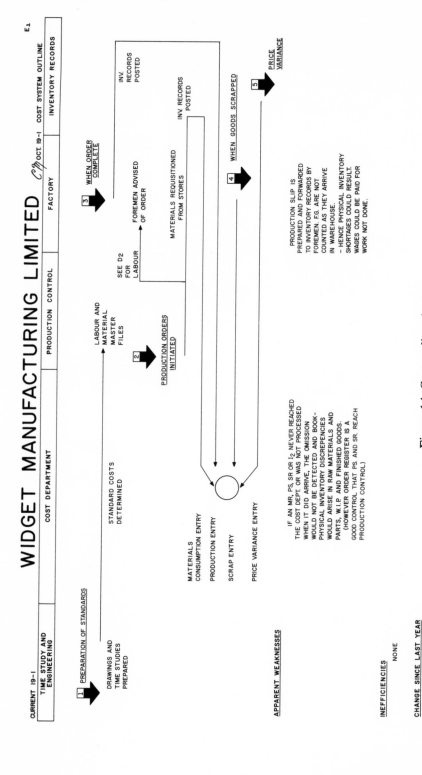

Figure 14. Cost outline chart.

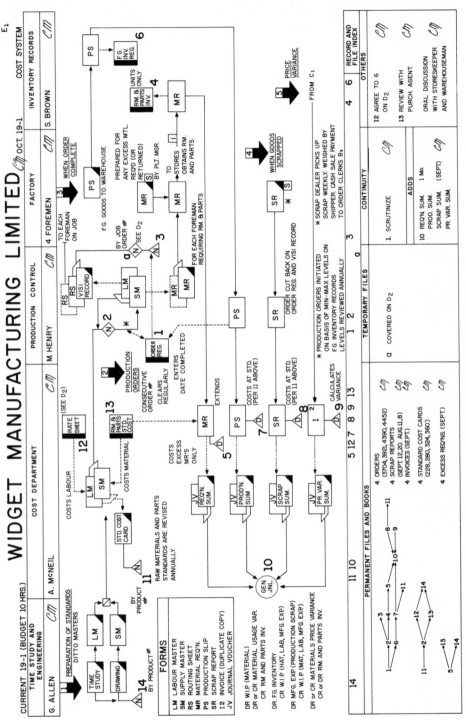

Figure 15. Cost flow chart.

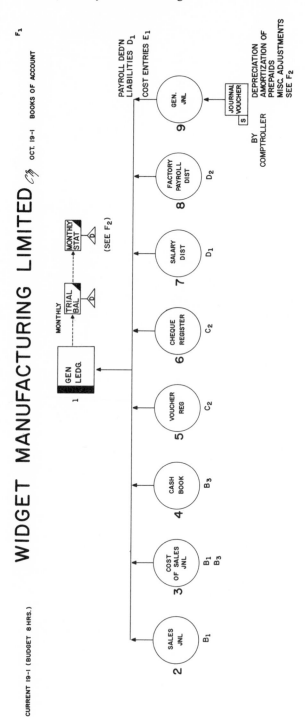

Figure 16. Chart of books of account.

CHAPTER

8

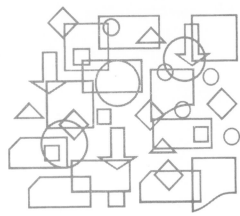

IMPROVING

CHARTING TECHNIQUES

The technique of flow charting was described in Chapter 4. Learning the symbols and the charting conventions is not difficult. But using the technique in the best way to produce the most readable and the most useful charts takes a little longer. This chapter reviews some of the common pitfalls in charting and suggests ways of avoiding them. These points, of course, are more important in first year analytical audits, where the flow charts are being prepared for the first time.

Clear Layout

One of the first requirements for a readable flow chart is a clear layout. The chart should have as straight an outline as possible and an easily visible flow. The success or failure of a flow chart in this respect can usually be seen at a glance from the related outline chart. Crossing lines should be avoided; however unambiguously the crossing is made, a chart with much of it appears far more complicated than it really is and rapidly induces fatigue in the reader. Among other things the avoidance of crossing lines means that the various books, ledgers and records must be charted in accessible positions so that the appropriate document flows can reach them easily. Finally, long meandering lines crossing from one side of the chart to the other should be avoided; they are confusing for the reader to follow if, in fact, he persists long enough to reach their final destination.

A brief example will help to illustrate the above points. The flow chart in Figure 17 contains reasonable information but it has been laid out very poorly. This visual confusion can be eliminated by rearranging the chart as shown in Figure 18. The long flow lines have been eliminated by rearranging the columns. Some of the crossing lines have been eliminated by bringing in documents both above and below the books (order register, accounts receivable ledger, and sales journal)—i.e. by placing the books

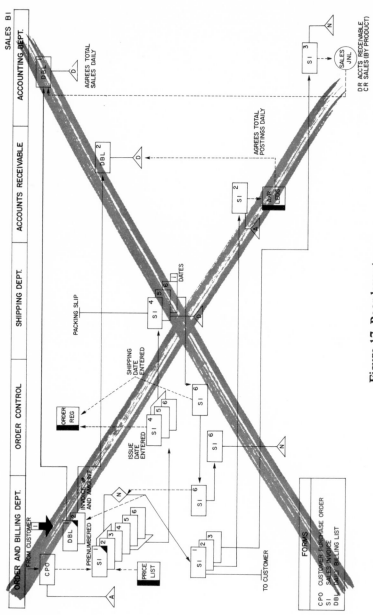

Figure 17. Poor layout.

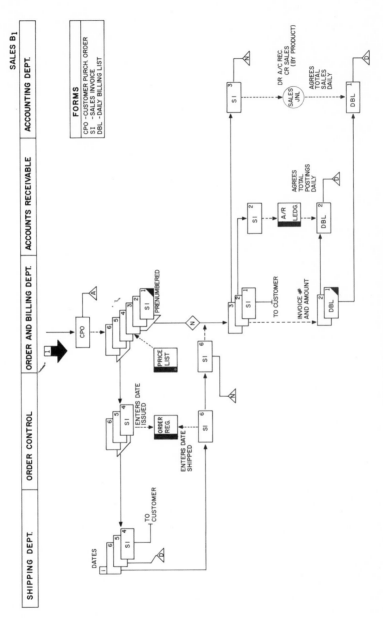

Figure 18. Improved layout.

in more accessible positions. The remaining crossing lines have been eliminated by a sensible arrangement of document flow. For instance, in the billing department SI_1, SI_2 and SI_3 need not cross SI_4, SI_5 and SI_6, and SI_2 need not cross SI_3. In the shipping department SI_5 need not cross SI_6 and SI_4 need not cross DBL_2.

It is sometimes difficult, of course, to determine in advance how a complicated flow chart should be set out. One way is by jotting down rough flow lines to see how the layout will appear. This can be done very quickly —although several attempts may have to be made before an easily visible, fairly straight flow is arrived at. For instance, Figure 19 contrasts the flow lines of the original flow chart in the above example with the flow lines of the improved flow chart. It can be seen immediately that the first layout is going to involve many crossing paths and that the order of steps leading from the start to the finish is hard to follow. The advantage of first trying out the flow lines in rough is that it avoids the situation in which a time-consuming detailed chart is completed before the poor layout is noticed. If the simple flow lines seem unclear the detailed flow chart is sure to be hopelessly confused.

Simplifying the Charts

Once the flow chart is rearranged into the optimum layout for usefulness and readability, the next most important thing is to keep the chart as simple as possible. All irrelevant information must be eliminated. For instance, on the flow chart of a payroll system none of the details of the annual preparation of T4 slips, the distribution of two copies to the employee and two copies to the government, and the method of filing the fifth copy are very relevant to an analysis of the regular payroll procedures and controls. To include them on the chart just uses up more space and complicates the chart without cause.

Sometimes certain procedures will be relevant but are charted in far too much detail. Unnecessary detail must be eliminated. For instance, the flow chart in Figure 20 can be reduced to the simple chart in Figure 21 with no real loss in information. The unnecessary details eliminated are: (a) temporary files of SO's in the order and shipping departments, (b) temporary file of SO_1's and SO_2's in the shipping department, (c) the note at the bottom of the order department column, (d) temporary file of invoices in the billing department, and (e) starting arrow number two and the related broken line.

Finally, there may be cases where the flow charts are unnecessarily repetitive. For instance, Figure 22 shows a chart where the system has been stratified into three different types of transactions. A second look, however, shows that many of the procedures for these three types are identical. Such repetition or stratification should be avoided. The flow chart can be consolidated and reduced to something of the format of

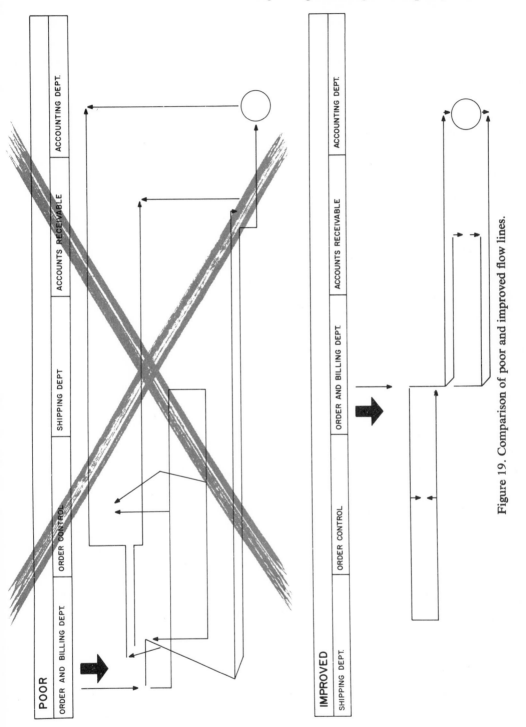

Figure 19. Comparison of poor and improved flow lines.

Figure 23. All material requisitions have been charted as one system except in areas where they are actually handled in a different manner. The foremen have been shown within the stores column. Finally, the three stores areas have been combined (and the fact that there are three areas merely disclosed by note).

Other Problems to be Avoided

There are three other important points for the auditor to bear in mind when charting. The first is to avoid *over*simplification; the second, to choose the best method of charting alternatives; the third, to find the best method of dividing a large system among several flow charts.

While the previous paragraphs have stressed the need for eliminating unnecessary detail and simplifying the charts wherever possible, the other extreme is also to be avoided. The auditor must not omit information which is essential in order to interpret the chart or which is crucial to the evaluation of control. For instance, in Figure 24 the reader cannot really tell what the system is. Are the work tickets really being used daily to complete the calculation of job costs and then being filed in a permanent file of old tickets? If so, some of the work tickets will be missing from the temporary file used to prepare the labour distribution at the month end. As a result, some labour would never be charged into production and work in progress would be understated. Conversely, are the work tickets really being held until the end of the month for the labour distribution and then being filed in employee number order with previous months' tickets? If so, previous months' tickets might periodically be missed in completing the job cost report. As a result, the entry relieving inventory would be incomplete and work in process would be overstated. Probably neither of these two rather obvious errors is occurring. But the point is that one cannot tell from the flow chart—and hence the chart is not fulfilling its function as a tool to analyze internal control. Figure 25 shows a corrected chart which removes the ambiguity. The reader might refer back to Figure 20 to satisfy himself why the charting of certain temporary files produced unnecessary detail there, while in Figure 24 the omission of certain temporary files introduced awkward ambiguity.

It was stated in Chapter 4 that there are three methods of handling alternative paths in a system. First, they can be charted by using a fork in either a solid or broken arrow. Secondly, the main system can be charted and the alternative explained by footnote. Thirdly, the alternative system can be recharted on a completely different chart. There are advantages and disadvantages to each approach. The first approach achieves the greatest concentration of information in one place—but sometimes at the price of complicating the chart unduly. The second approach keeps the charting simple—but sometimes at the price of obscuring important procedures by an unduly cumbersome footnote. The third approach avoids the first two problems—but sometimes at the price of charting in several places procedures which are common to all the alternatives. It is a matter of judgment and experience which method of handling the alternative is best in a given situation. Figure 26 shows an example of what a consistently wrong choice can produce. Figure 27 shows the same chart reorganized more efficiently. The alternatives in the order department are better handled by a separate chart than by crowding on the same chart. The alternatives in the billing department are better handled by a footnote than by the forked arrow. The alternatives in the accounts receivable and accounting departments disappear. The alternatives in the cost department are better handled by a forked arrow than by a long footnote (which contains important documents and a posting source to the general ledger which is somewhat hidden in the original chart).

When a system will require eleven columns to chart and the auditor can fit only six columns of information on each charting page, he must make a decision as to how he will split the system into pieces which will each fit logically on one page. This was discussed in Chapter 4. But making the division in the best way requires careful judgment. The division should be made in such a way that the amount of inter-chart referencing (documents flowing from one chart to another) is minimized. The outline charts in Figure 28 illustrated a poor division. The charter had attempted to cover the procedures leading up to the purchase entry on one chart and those leading up to the payment entry on a second. When the receiving procedures could not be fitted on the first chart he placed them on a third chart. A better arrangement would have been that shown in Figure 29. This cannot, of course, be taken as a model. Every situation is different, the amount of necessary detail and therefore the charting space required is different, and accordingly the optimum method of division into several charts will be different.

Importance of Readable Charts

The foregoing examples have covered the most common obstacles to good charting. If the auditor employing charting will guard against these carefully, he will find his charts are readable and easy to use. There is no question that it takes slightly longer (in the first year) to produce a simple, clear chart than to produce a complicated, confusing one. The charter must remember that the confusion may seem slight to him—but only because at the conclusion of the audit he knows the systems thoroughly. Of course he will understand his own charts. But will the reviewer or the audit staff a year from now be able to understand them? It is not enough for the charts to be accurate: they must also be presented in a clear and readable fashion. Flow charting is a means of communication and it is worth taking a little longer in the first year to ensure that they can, in fact, communicate.

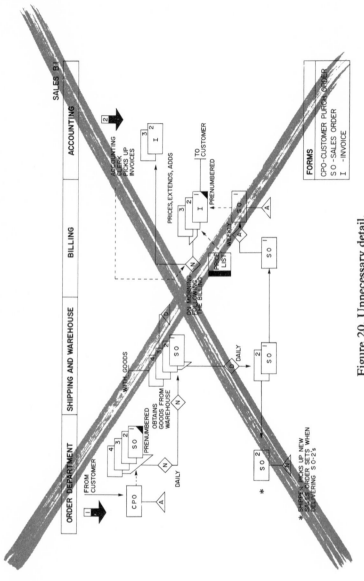

Figure 20. Unnecessary detail.

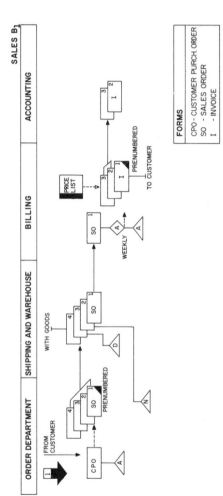

Figure 21. Unnecessary detail removed.

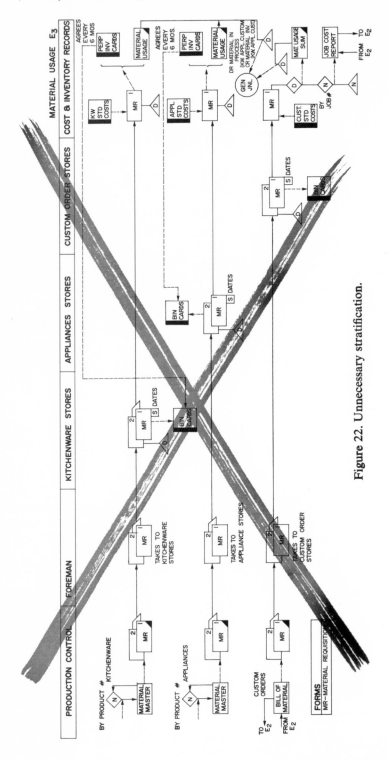

Figure 22. Unnecessary stratification.

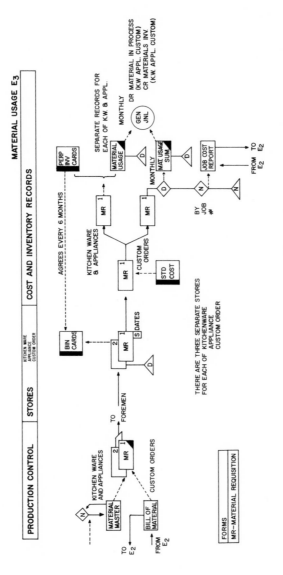

Figure 23. Unnecessary stratification eliminated.

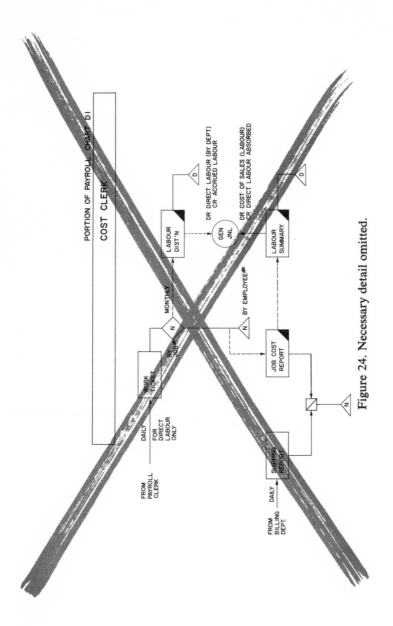

Figure 24. Necessary detail omitted.

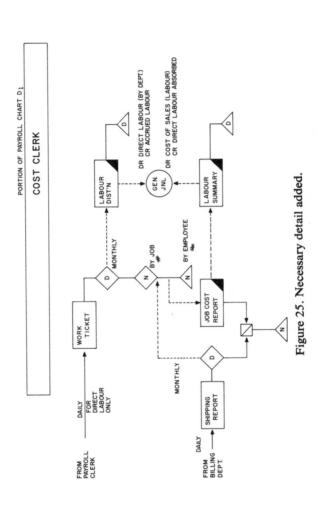

Figure 25. Necessary detail added.

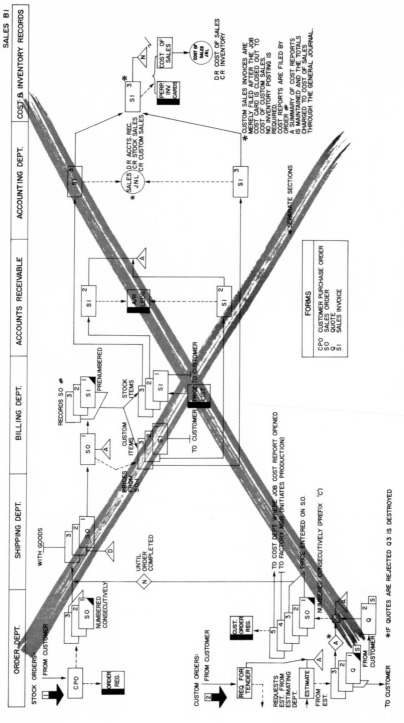

Figure 26. Poor treatment of alternatives.

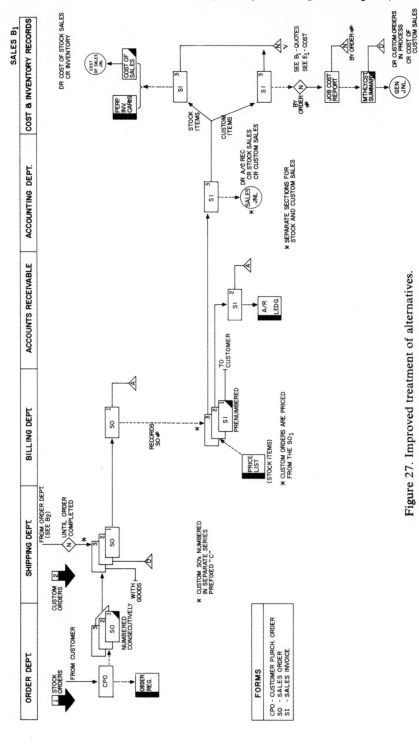

Figure 27. Improved treatment of alternatives.

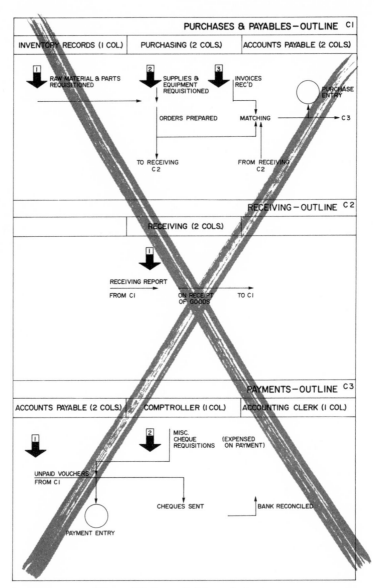

Figure 28. Poor division of charts.

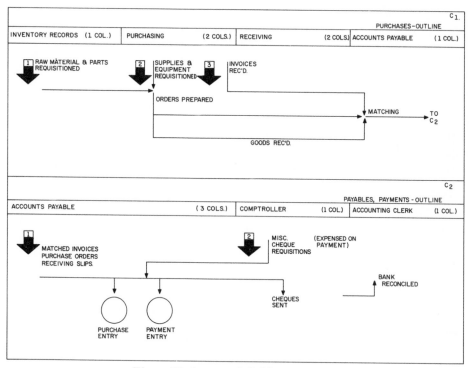

Figure 29. Improved division of charts.

CHAPTER

9

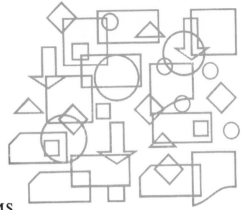

APPLICATION TO

PUNCHED CARD

AND COMPUTER SYSTEMS

The larger the organization and the greater the volume of transactions the greater the savings which should accrue from the use of a systems-oriented auditing approach. Checking all transactions for a specified test period becomes excessively time-consuming while, on the other hand, the system of internal control is likely to be stronger and therefore to repay more generously a thorough analysis of control. But large organizations are the very ones most apt to have punched card or computer applications. Can analytical auditing be adapted to these data processing systems? The answer is that it can. In fact, such systems are model subjects for this type of audit. In data processing installations the procedures are more formalized, the systems more reproducible. If auditing "through the system" makes sense for a manual system, it makes even more sense for a punched card or computer system. Certain modifications of the audit steps described in Chapters 5 and 6 are, however, desirable. These modifications are outlined in the present chapter.

Flow Charting for Punched Card Systems

The principles of flow charting for punched card systems are the same as for manual systems. Every punched card system, however, involves a considerable amount of card handling, transferring, collating, merging, and sorting which is of lesser importance to internal control as such. From a control point of view, the crucial steps are when information is punched into a card or when printed or other output is produced from a card (although, of course, controls over the improper insertion or omission of cards during processing are also important). The auditor is not undertaking an elaborate study of machine utilization (which would require detailed charts showing all these steps) but rather an analysis of internal con-

121

trol. He must, therefore, distinguish between these crucial controls and the mere mechanics of the intermediate card handling. The charting of the mechanics must be minimized if the flow charts of punched card systems are not to become hopelessly cumbersome. In general, the auditor's flow charts (directed toward control analysis) will be less detailed than the typical flow charts of systems analysts (prepared when designing the detailed procedures for the punched card department).

With the foregoing caution, the charting of punched card operations can now be discussed. A few additional symbols are useful to show the various punched cards and tabulated reports which will be of importance in the systems analysis and in the walk-through audit.

This symbol is the conventional one for a punched card.

The normal symbol for a print-out or run from a punched card tabulating machine is convenient to use since it is awkward to classify such a run as either a "document" or a "permanent book or record."

Here an order card (OC) is being keypunched (and verified) from a sales order document (SO) which is then filed alphabetically. In most cases, however, the keypunching operation must be described somewhat more fully in order to show the operation of control totals and the review of document authorizations, important elements in the overall system of internal control. Figure 30 illustrates a more complete chart on a keypunching operation. There, a group printing of each batch of punched cards is made and the resulting print-out of control totals is agreed to the control totals submitted by the source department along with the corresponding batch of source documents. This proves that a source document has not been mislaid or incorrectly keypunched. In addition, all detail

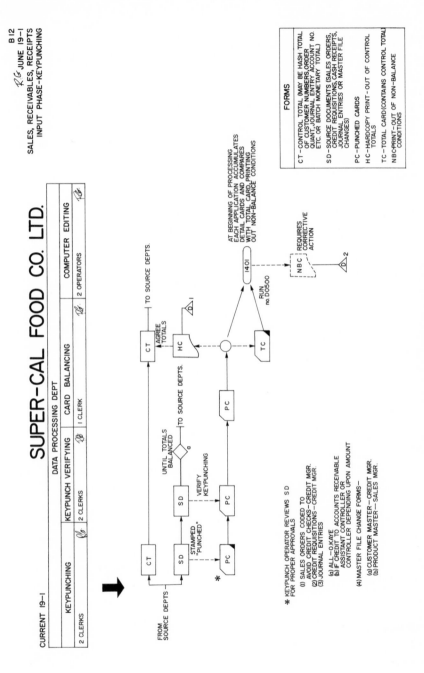

Figure 30. Keypunching.

cards are balanced to a total card before or during each run. This proves that a punched card has not been mislaid, incorrectly read or inadvertently added to the deck.

Where it is necessary to show a deck of punched cards this conventional symbol can be used. However, if the charting of collating, sorting, and merging operations is kept to a minimum (as suggested above) it will often be unnecessary to draw a deck of cards: a single card will be understood to represent a deck wherever the processing would obviously be done in a batch.

Thus, here a sales summary is being produced from a deck of cards on a tabulating machine. Sometimes it is convenient to show the process of tabulation simply by the broken arrow as used here. At other times, where a variety of output is being produced all from the same deck of punched cards at once it may be desirable to indicate the machine processing more explicitly.

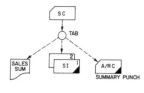

Thus, here a sales summary, the sales invoices, and summary-punched accounts receivable cards are all produced from the deck of sales cards. Only where master decks (e.g. product cost cards or customer name-and-address cards) or tub files of prepunched cards (e.g. order cards prepunched except for quantity) are involved is it usually necessary to draw the cards as a deck to avoid ambiguity.

It has been stressed that excessive detail in the charting of punched card operations must be avoided. Now that the individual symbols have been discussed, an example of unnecessary detail can be examined. **Figure 31** shows two methods of charting a small part of a sales system:

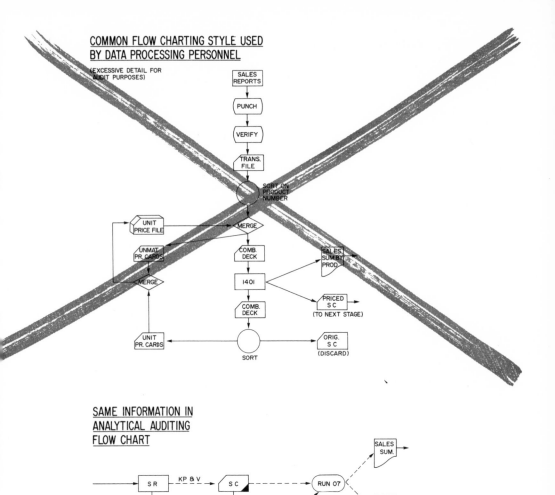

Figure 31. Two charting styles.

the pricing of sales reports and the preparation of a sales summary. It can be seen that one of the flow charting styles in common use among data processing personnel, while well adapted to their purposes, provides more detail than is required for audit purposes. The analytical auditing style conveys essentially the same information in considerably less space. (This is just an arbitrary example; in both cases, some important information is missing respecting control totals—as was shown in Figure 30.)

The previous examples have illustrated only small parts of a system. Figure 32 shows a more complete flow chart for an order and billing system using punched cards. The related outline chart is shown in Figure 33 and notes a number of weaknesses and inefficiencies which may be observed in the system. It can be seen, then, that the flow charting of

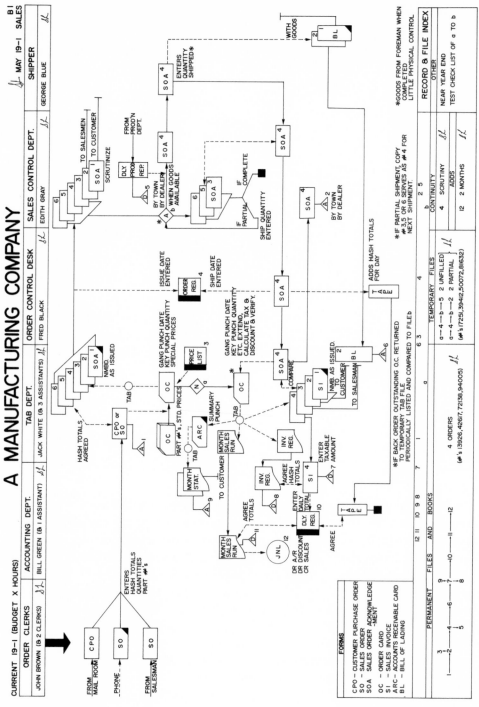

Figure 32. Punched card flow chart.

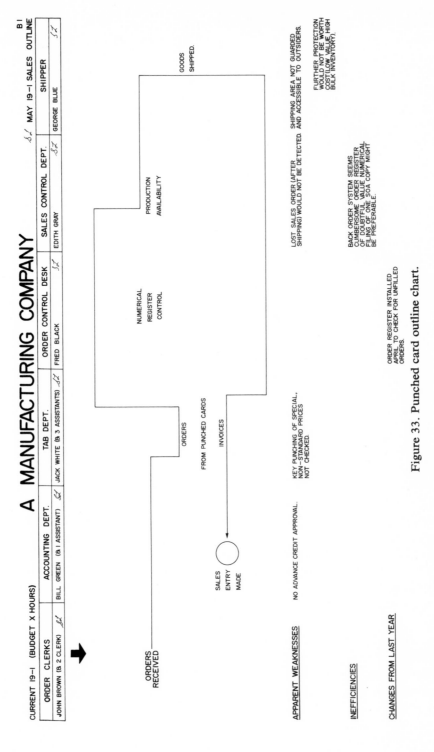

Figure 33. Punched card outline chart.

punched card systems is not essentially different from the flow charting of manual systems. In analyzing the control, however, there will be a number of control features which are peculiar to punched card systems. To ensure that these are not overlooked it may be desirable for the auditor to supplement the basic control questions (Appendix III) with a more detailed punched card check list. A number of such check lists have been described in recent articles but a discussion of all these special control features is beyond the scope of this book.

Computer Systems

While punched card systems do not present the auditor with any fundamental problems not common to manual systems, with computer systems the situation is different. Computers have a much greater influence on the nature of the accounting and management reporting system surrounding them. In addition, they involve a considerable number of logical decisions and important controls within the actual internal processing of the computer. It is not the purpose of this book to give an extensive description of all the audit techniques which may be appropriate for particular computer systems. This would necessitate a discussion of each control feature in an EDP system and a consideration of when and how special techniques such as the use of test decks or tape dumps should be applied. The intention in this chapter is merely to demonstrate how the analytical auditing approach can be generally adapted to the audit of computer systems.

Three general premises should be stated at the outset. First, the computer is an integral part of the total accounting system and must therefore be considered in the context of the system of which it is a part. The computer hardware and personnel provide processing services for many departments and for many different kinds of information. However, as each type of data is processed, the computer uses programs and is operated under instructions specifically designed for that transaction type and so the computer becomes inextricably part of the total system of processing for that particular type of information. For each type of transaction the computer must therefore be looked at in conjunction with all the other operations performed on the data. A so-called "computer audit" designed to treat the computer as a separate and independent entity cannot lead to an intelligent evaluation of the total control system. Secondly, if the computer is part of the system, then a systems-oriented approach (such as analytical auditing) can, with certain modifications, be used to audit it. Thirdly, the auditor does not have to be able to read program logic or "block diagrams" in order to perform the audit—although a limited background knowledge of how computers work and what they can do is an advantage. This last premise, perhaps the most contentious one, will be further examined on the following pages.

Flow Charting for Computer Systems

In computer systems, unlike manual or even punched card systems, a considerable amount of processing, analyzing, comparing, decision-making, and checking takes place *within the computer*. Much of this internal processing, and the controls built into it, must be of concern to the auditor. In other words, the auditor must consider two systems: the *internal system* (which goes on inside the computer) and the *external system* (which goes on outside the computer). This necessarily leads to some modifications in flow charting techniques when applied to EDP systems. The external system in part lends itself to the same type of flow charting as described in previous chapters. This is examined in more detail below. The internal system requires different treatment. EDP personnel customarily document the internal logic of a computer program by means of "block diagrams." Block diagrams, however, are too detailed for what the auditor needs to know and so a different alternative for the auditor is suggested (see page 135).

Because of the division of a computer system into internal systems (or EDP phases) and external systems (or manual phases), the whole system is often more difficult to visualize, and yet it is important that the system be seen as a whole. The auditor, as has been said, cannot split the computer out from the rest of the system for a special "computer audit." Rather he must follow the normal analytical audit plan and consider each section (such as sales-receivables-receipts) as a unit—even though it involves both manual and computer phases. For this reason a summary chart, such as shown in Figure 34, is usually helpful. In this particular example customers' orders, journal entries and cash receipts data flow into the computer department and produce: first, invoices to the customer (operation 05); secondly, an up-dated accounts receivable "ledger" on magnetic tape (operation 06); and thirdly, an up-dated general ledger and monthly accounting report (operation 08). Of course, each of these three operations includes a large number of separate computer runs—and these complexities are not indicated on the summary chart. Although the chart is, therefore, over-simplified it does help the auditor to understand the system before becoming embroiled in the details. It is also of assistance to persons reviewing the file or conducting the audit the following year.

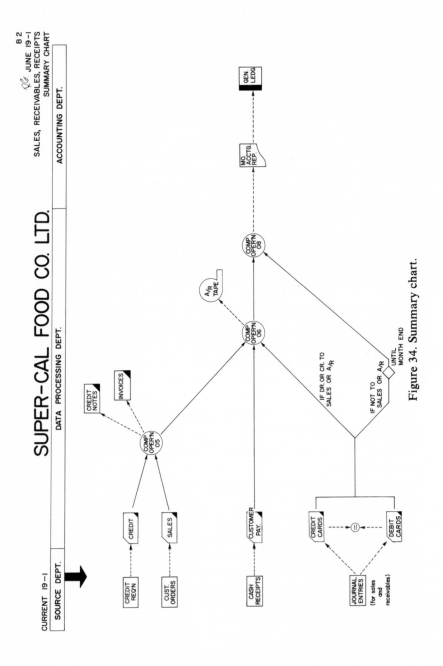

Figure 34. Summary chart.

In a manual accounting system the flow charting is best accomplished if each sheet of paper is transaction-oriented. That is, each page is devoted to a type of transaction and how that transaction is treated. For example, separate charts may be prepared for domestic and export sales; for wholesale and retail receivables; for branch and head office receipts. In a system employing a computer, however, all types of transactions are usually processed by the computer at some point and it is easier to chart all the computer processing (for that sub-system) in one place. For charting purposes it is therefore useful to break each sub-system into compartments or phases rather than into transaction types. A common breakdown is:

(1) input phase—the flow of data from the point of transaction origination to the point of last visible input into the computer (i.e.—to preparation of magnetic tape or punched cards);

(2) processing phase—the flow of data through the computer (this phase is left uncharted for the moment);

(3) output phase—the flow of data from first visible output from the computer to final posting of the data in the general ledger.

Therefore, after completing the summary chart, the auditor can prepare normal analytical-audit flow charts for the external phases of the sub-system: (a) from original recording of transaction to last visible computer input and (b) from point of first visible computer output to general ledger. In the output phase, the charting should be restricted initially to "primary output"—that is, actual accounting records or supporting data as distinguished from "secondary output" such as exception reports, error listings, statistical information, etc. The secondary output can be charted later on a selective basis. Meanwhile the flow charts should be left in rough form.

Figure 35 illustrates the input phase for cash receipts and journal entries (for the same system as summarized in Figure 34) up to the point of punched cards being passed to the computer processing phase. Likewise, Figures 36 and 37 illustrate output phase flow charts: the former showing the distribution of sales invoices received from the processing phase; the latter showing the generation of entries for the general ledger. Usually it is convenient to chart the pre-EDP (input) phase and the post-EDP (output) phase separately in this way. Occasionally, however, it may be simpler to combine them on the same flow charts, leaving a slight gap to indicate where the EDP phase occurs. Sometimes a fourth phase, "communications," may be useful when data is collected at regional points and transmitted to a central processing location.

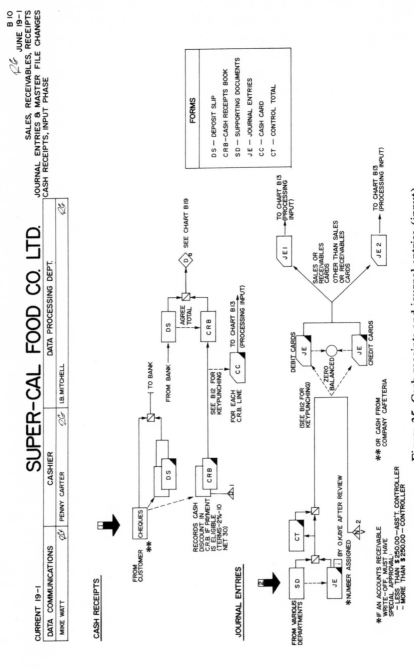

Figure 35. Cash receipts and journal entries (input).

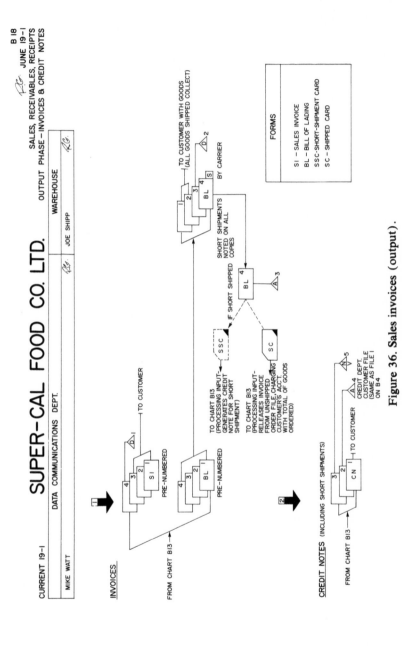

Figure 36. Sales invoices (output).

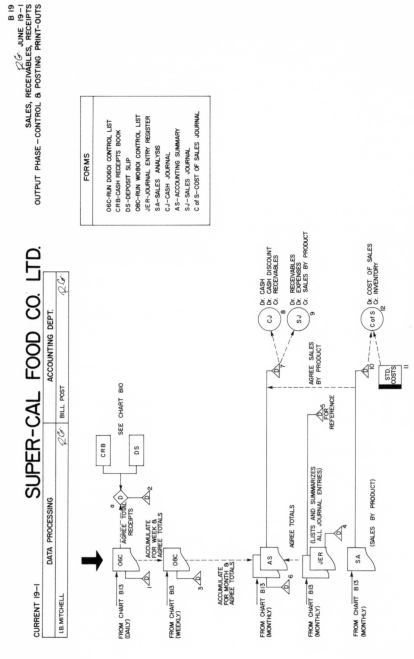

Figure 37. Accounting entries (output).

Summarizing the EDP Processing Phase

What the auditor requires is a broad picture of the EDP phase. He already knows where the *input* comes from and where the *output* goes—from his flow charts of the external system. He needs, therefore, some form of computer phase chart which shows the principal operations in getting from one to the other—though not necessarily showing every machine run individually. An example of such a chart is shown in Figure 38. The chart should show, in summary form, the path from last visible input to first visible output—that is, the gap in the flow charts of the external system (to which the computer phase chart can be referenced). Thus, in Figure 38 the computer input is referenced to the input charts B_9 to B_{12} and the computer output is referenced to the output charts B_{17} to B_{20}.

The ease with which this chart can be prepared will depend upon the computer documentation that the client has. Documentation will vary widely from one client to another. Some will have lengthy narrative explanations of the purpose, input and output of each individual run. Others will have various types of flow charts and block diagrams with varying degrees of detail. And some will have both the foregoing and, as well, summary charts comparable to Figure 38. In the last case the auditor can adapt the client's charts directly to his needs. Unfortunately, the majority of clients will probably not have a suitable summary chart; in these cases the auditor will have to prepare his own summary—usually after a review of the operators' run manuals or a discussion with the client's programmers.

If a suitable summary chart is not available, a run structure analysis similar to Figure 39 can be prepared without too much difficulty as an intermediate step. A review of the client's available documentation (i.e. block diagrams or operators' run manuals) enables the auditor to chart the important runs, remembering that the sorting and merging operations are seldom of significance to the auditor. This run structure analysis provides a basic understanding of the relationship of the computer runs or groups of runs. Study of Figure 39 will show that each computer run (or a group of related runs) is represented by a circle and the connecting lines indicate the processing pattern. For better understanding, primary output and useful secondary output are added to this working paper, using the broken arrow convention to indicate the preparation of documents.

Once this analysis has been completed, the EDP processing can be divided into logical sections and summarized in a manner similar to Figure 38. The division should be fairly obvious after the auditor's review and discussion. For example, in Figures 38 and 39 all billing work is completed before the accounts receivable are posted. Thus there is a clear

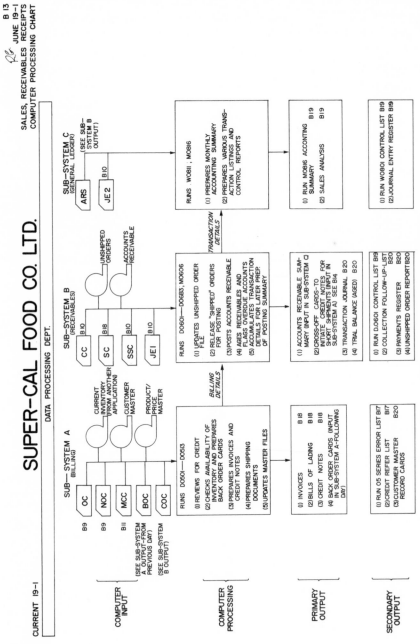

Figure 38. Computer processing phase.

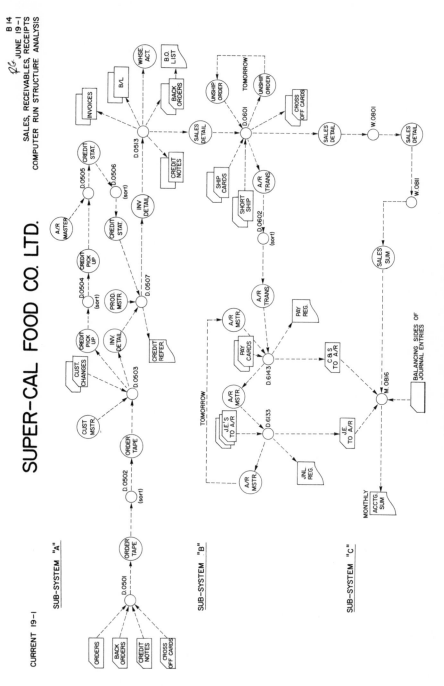

Figure 39. Run structure analysis.

division between billing and posting. The monthly summarization of transactions also forms a separate operation. Therefore, grouping of all the separate runs into three main divisions is appropriate. In a payroll application the processing may also fall into three categories: calculation of gross pay; calculation of net pay and preparation of cheques; and monthly summarization. In any application a convenient division will be readily apparent. The addition of input and output documents and their referencing to the external system flow charts completes the charting of the EDP processing phase.

It is worth emphasizing that in preparing the charts summarizing the computer processing phase, the auditor must steer a course between two extremes. In the first place, he must avoid making so generalized a schedule that it shows nothing about the EDP processing at all. That is, it is not sufficient to show merely the input entering the computer room and the total output coming out, leaving the rest to a mysterious black box which somehow converts the one into the other. This much has already been shown, in any case, on the summary chart for the whole section. But it does not provide an understanding of the processing function or permit an evaluation of the internal control. In the second place, the auditor must avoid making so detailed an analysis that it leads him into all the intricate mechanics *within* each computer run. Such an analysis would take in the logic block diagrams of every program and would be extremely complicated and time-consuming. What is required here is an understanding of the relationships *between* the different runs but not an exhaustive analysis of the program structure *within* each run—though it is, of course, necessary to have a general knowledge of what each run is doing. A consideration of the relationships between the different runs should provide all the information needed to understand the system from an audit point of view and to search intelligently for controls.

Effect of a Computer System on Internal Control

The presence of a computer in an accounting system always has a significant effect on internal control. Typically in a computer system there will be changes in the *external system* because fewer people will be involved in handling the paper work. The resulting lack of visual review or *editing by people* in the *external system* may or may not be compensated for by programmed controls or *editing by the computer* in the *internal system*. Also, new features will be found in the external system—batching, card count reconciliation, tape storage procedures, etc.—which do not occur in a manual system. The evaluation of the control in any computer system must comprise both a review of the changed control in the external system and an investigation of the new controls in the internal system. Clearly, then, the computer processing must be examined as an integral part of each sub-system when conducting the audit. The goal should be a complete documentation of the internal control evalution and of the audit procedures performed to prove this control for each sub-system as a unit (including both manual and computer phases).

To begin with, the internal controls in computer systems can be divided into three different types. This in itself makes the evaluation of control somewhat different from manual systems. First, there are the relatively few, but extremely important *hardware controls*[1] which are built into the computer by the manufacturer. By detecting invalid characters, reading errors, internal transfer errors, overflow conditions and output writing errors, these controls are designed to insure the accuracy of internal processing.

Secondly, there are the *programmed controls* which are designed for a particular computer run by the programmer and incorporated into the program. These controls test the data (both the input and the computed results) for various conditions as it is being processed. The number of programmed controls in a given application will vary with the type of application, the sophistication of the computer system, the imagination of the programmer and the philosophy of the company. (Programmed controls are complementary to external peripheral controls—see below; many key controls can be either peripheral or programmed and as long as they are present it does not matter from a control point of view which type they are.) Programmed controls include limit checks, range checks, compatability checks, reasonability checks, etc. For instance, a programmed control might check that the gross profit on each sale fell within a predetermined range—thus providing a safeguard against obvious pricing errors.

Finally, there are the *peripheral controls* relating to the systems and procedures external to the computer. They encompass traditional controls associated with a manual system and, in addition, controls over the actual operation of the computer. The peripheral controls can be classified under such headings as: division of duties, preparation of input, control of output, machine operation, and other controls. While some of these divisons sound familiar, many of the details are new for a computer system (for instance, division of duties includes the segregation of programmers and operators).

---

[1]Some of the more common of these controls are parity checks, validity checks, double reading checks, and echo checks.

Analysis of Controls

The "traditional" peripheral procedural controls associated with the manual phases of the system can generally be seen from an analysis of the normal flow charts of the external system and verified by the methods described in Chapter 5. However, many of the control features governing the actual operation of the computer are different enough from those of a manual system that it is useful to supplement the basic reminder questions (Appendix III) with a more detailed computer check list. These operating controls can usually be verified by observation.

The hardware controls cannot, of course, be seen on the flow charts of the external system. They can be most easily identified and verified by reviewing the manufacturer's literature with the guidance of a computer check list to focus attention on the important controls. Unlike the other types of controls, hardware controls do not have to be verified and evaluated for each application. They are unchanging from job to job and are therefore common to all applications.

The programmed controls, finally, are the most difficult to assess. How are they to be determined and their existence in the computer program proved? Theoretically, one could find all the programmed controls by reading the detailed print-outs or block diagrams of the program. However, both would be time-consuming, the former would require the ability to read program language, and the latter *would afford no proof that the block diagram being read was the same as the actual program used in the computer.*

All programmed controls, however, have one thing in common: when the data violates the controlled condition—that is, it exceeds the limit, it falls outside the range, it is invalid or it is subject to special conditions— a signal of some nature will indicate that a possible error or an unacceptable condition has been detected in the input. This signal may be output in the form of error listings on paper, error reports on magnetic tape or exception cards—or it may be a machine halt. In any case, it can be designated as "secondary output" to distinguish it from "primary output" such as sales invoices or accounting entries. It is this common characteristic of producing some form of secondary output that is useful in identifying (and in later verifying the operation of) the necessary programmed controls.

In a manual system control evaluation is done by examining the flow charts, bearing in mind the key internal control reminder questions, observing the strengths and weaknesses, and then assessing their cumulative effect. One could, by analogy, approach a computer system by making a complete inventory of all existing programmed controls followed by an evaluation of the list thus obtained. Such an approach, however, would be extremely laborious. The auditor would have to study thoroughly the program logic of every computer run. After all this, much of the work would turn out to be unnecessary, since many of the programmed controls are not crucial to the accuracy of the output. Many, for instance, are involved with catching at a convenient time (in order to avoid delays in subsequent programs) an error which would in any case have been caught later. Detecting a transaction record out of sequence would be an example. These types of controls are important for maximum computer efficiency but they are not essential as far as accounting accuracy is involved and they need not be examined or evaluated by the auditor. The auditor will save time, therefore, if he confines his attention to the smaller number of "necessary controls."

For this reason, it is more efficient in a computer system to proceed not by listing all the controls present and then evaluating them, but by deciding what controls are necessary and then seeing if they are present. Deciding what controls are necessary is equivalent to *preparing a detailed internal control questionnaire* directed at the specific system under review. In the analytical audit of a manual system it was suggested that brief reminder questions (as in Appendix III) were more efficient and more flexible than lengthy *standard* questionnaires. This was because the auditor's review consisted there of observation of all controls followed by assessment of their cumulative effect. With computer systems, however, if the auditor's review consists of decisions as to controls required followed by a search for these controls, then a comprehensive questionnaire must be the starting point. The questionnaire in this case, of course, is not a predetermined one but a questionnaire prepared by the auditor *for the specific system under review*. For a small manual system the time required to produce a tailor-made questionnaire would not be justified. For a large computer system, however, the time to prepare such a questionnaire will be small in comparison to the rest of the systems audit and in comparison to the time required to identify, verify and evaluate all the existing programmed controls.

In preparing a comprehensive list of the control features he believes to be necessary, the auditor can be guided by the key reminder questions for the appropriate section (such as sales-receivables-receipts) and also by his knowledge of the actual system of his client. However, since there are a number of control features which are peculiar to computer systems some additional EDP check list is desirable. Again it is not within the scope of this book to review such a check list or all the special control features in

SUPER-CAL FOOD CO. LTD.

CURRENT 19–1

B16
RG. JUNE 19–1
SALES, RECEIVABLES, RECEIPTS
PROGRAMMED CONTROLS AUDIT

Control Feature	Physical Evidence	Required Audit (1) Agree error condition with original input and determine cause	(2) Establish that data was rejected from system	(3) Follow up correction of erroneous data	Extent	Initial
1. Daily edit run D0500 accumulates various control totals from the detailed transaction data and compares these totals with manually calculated totals to ensure that all input has been fed into the computer for processing.	Run D0500 print-out "Non-balance conditions"	B12.2 → B12.1 Note: B12.2 was reviewed but apparently there had been no errors during the last 12 months. Therefore on a surprise basis we attended the daily edit processing and withheld 2 input punched cards from 1 batch of each type of input. We controlled the print-out of non-balance conditions and reconciled the resulting control totals with the cards processed and cards withheld. We concluded that the programmed control was functioning properly.	N/A—See note below	N/A	4 non-balance conditions	RG
2. Each order is checked to the customer master to ensure that it is for an existing customer.	Run D0503 error list "No master record"	B17.1 → B20.7 (There should not be a CMRC in B20.7.)	B17.1 → B20.1 (There should be no record of the order on the TJ for that date.)	B17.1 → B17.4 (There should be a corrected SO.)	4 rejected orders	RG
3. "Charge to" and "ship to" addresses on order and master file are compared. If these do not agree, the order is rejected.	Run D0503 error list "No order header"	B17.1 → B20.7 (addresses should not agree.)	As above	As above	4 rejected orders	RG
4. Product codes on order are compared with product master and orders with invalid codes are rejected.	Run D0501 error list "Incorrect product"	B17.1 → product code list in Sales Dept. (There should be no such codes.)	As above	As above	4 rejected orders	RG
5. Each order is compared with the customer master. The following conditions are flagged and the orders rejected: (a) order puts customer's account over credit limit	Run D0505 credit referral list	B17.3 → B20.1 → B20.7 (Balance per TJ plus current SO should exceed credit limit per CMRC.)	B17.3 → B20.1 (There should be no record of the order on the TJ for that date.)	B17.3 → B17.4 (Only if order not rejected. Check for special credit code and credit manager's signature.)	4 rejected orders	RG
(b) account is overdue	"Account overdue"	B17.3 → B20.1 (Account should be overdue.)	As above	As above	4 rejected orders	RG
(c) account is on a "referral," or "single order" basis	"Referral" or "single order"	B17.3 → B20.7 (Check credit status.)	As above	As above	4 rejected orders	RG
6. Extensions and additions on each credit note are checked and errors flagged.	Run D0504 error list "non-add"	B17.1 → B9.1	B17.1 → B20.1 (There should be no record of credit on the TJ for that date.)	B17.1 → B9.1 → B18.4 (There should be a corrected CR and a CN.)	4 rejected credit notes	RG
7. Each cash receipt is matched against unpaid invoices in the customer's account. If the payment cannot be matched against an invoice it is flagged (but posted to the customer's account).	Payment register	B20.6 → B20.1	N/A	B20.6 → B10.2 (Vouch correcting journal entry if applicable.)	4 payments reported	RG
8. Orders remaining in unshipped order file for more than 5 days are flagged.	Unshipped order report	B20.6 → B17.4	N/A	Follow up reason for shipping delay.	4 unshipped orders reported	RG
9. Review of errors statistics for control features 2 to 8 listed above.		There was a consistent and reasonable pattern in each case except for control 5(a)—"over credit limit". There was a significant decline in the frequency of errors in April and May. This was explained by the increase in credit limits effective April 1, 19–1 as a result of a credit policy review.			January to May / June to December	RG

Figure 40. Audit of programmed controls.

detail. A number of such check lists have been described in recent articles.[2] The use of such a check list can help the auditor to recall all the possibilities of programmed and peripheral controls which may be relevant when he is preparing his detailed questionnaire.

Searching for Programmed Controls

In searching for all the controls which he has decided are essential to a satisfactory system (and which he has listed on his detailed questionnaire) the auditor should look first to the external system. Controls in the external system are the easiest to identify. When all answers yielded by his flow charts of the external system have been exhausted, any remaining unanswered questions represent controls which must be found among the programmed controls. This avoids wasting audit time on those programmed controls which are not crucial to the accounting accuracy (as mentioned before). In a simple computer system most of the necessary controls will be found in the external system and little will remain to be sought for in the programs. However, the more sophisticated and integrated the computer application is, the more questions one would expect to remain unanswered by the external system and to be satisfied by some programmed control.

Programmed controls, by their very nature, are not apparent from the flow charts. Therefore, as each necessary programmed control is identified it should be recorded on a special working paper. Figure 40 illustrates a convenient format that accommodates both a description of the control and the audit procedures required to verify it. The verification of these controls is discussed in the following pages.

Because programmed controls cause error reports or other physical evidence to be produced whenever an unacceptable condition (i.e. a "violation") is encountered, the easiest way to find programmed controls is to examine the different types of error conditions being reported on the secondary output. It is then possible to determine what controls *appear* to be exercised by the program. By employing the knowledge gained in preparing the computer processing chart, the search for a particular control can be directed to the secondary output of the most probable computer runs. The secondary print-outs that are used in identifying controls are important control documents and should therefore be added to the output flow charts. It is not enough for the auditor to know that errors are being properly reported on these print-outs. It is important for him to know that an adequate follow-up and correction system exists.

[2]See, for example, "An Internal Control Checklist for EDP" by H. B. Joplin in the July-August 1964 issue of *Management Services*.

Of course, if the necessary control still cannot be found among the programmed controls, a weakness exists. The auditor must then plan what appropriate weakness investigation he must carry out—just as in any analytical audit. For instance, the auditor will want to see that there is some safeguard against shipping goods to a bad credit risk. He will look first to the external system to see if some credit approval must be given to sales orders before they are passed to the computer room for key punching and processing. If no credit check is found in the external system then he will hope that some programmed control will cover the same point. A limit check could cause orders to be rejected when they would place the customer's account over a predetermined credit limit. If he finds no such programmed control, however, he must conclude that goods can in fact be shipped to bad credit risks. He must then, as in any analytical audit, decide what additional work he must do to satisfy himself that there are no serious problems within the accounts receivable because of this weakness.

Proving the Existence of Programmed Controls

Once the auditor has located essential programmed controls he must design audit procedures to prove: (a) the existence and operation of the necessary programmed controls; (b) the operation of prescribed procedures for correcting the erroneous data; (c) the reasonableness of the error frequency. The identification procedures discussed above do not prove that the controls are actually exercised on the processed data or that the control features are exactly as purported to be. Both of these points can be established by examining historical input data that violated the necessary controls. Thus, the auditor can select four examples from the secondary output evidencing apparent operation of the control and check these back to the original source documents to see that the original data was, in fact, in error—or in violation of the control condition (e.g. order exceeding credit limit, overdue account requiring follow-up, etc.)

The reliability of EDP equipment and the freedom of computers from external influence[3] (i.e.—they operate from stored programs of instructions) enable the auditor to conclude from this limited test that all data is subjected to the same control conditions. Of course the auditor must be careful not to over-generalize his conclusions too quickly. Both the secondary output and the source documents being examined in the above test must be carefully studied for any indication of a selective control feature. For instance, the secondary output might, on closer examination, reveal

[3]This assumes that the auditor has reviewed the peripheral controls surrounding the operation of the computer and found them to be satisfactory.

that only export orders were subject to the control. Alternatively, the coding spaces provided on the source documents, or discussions with EDP personnel, might reveal that certain controls can be by-passed. For instance, the credit manager's initials on the order might authorize a special punch in the card which instructs the computer to omit the credit check. The auditor should also be satisfied that the control level of various range and limit checks (for example $1,000) is approximately the amount he has been told. He should review the selected violations, and others if necessary, to find examples of violations which are close to the purported level of control.

Having proved the existence of the programmed control, the auditor can establish that prescribed procedures are operating to correct the erroneous data by tracing the same four examples through to their ultimate correction. Data which violates a programmed control may or may not be rejected from further processing. If the data is supposed to be rejected, the primary output must be examined to see that rejection did occur and the erroneous data does not appear on the primary output. The erroneous source documents must then be examined for the appropriate corrections and the corrected data traced to subsequent primary output. If the data is not supposed to be rejected, it must be traced to the appropriate primary output and evidence must be examined that these violations were reviewed and any required action taken.

To prove that the error frequency is reasonable, the auditor can review any available statistics summarizing the frequency of the various errors and other control violations by transaction type, by division, by month, etc. (Where statistics are not kept it will be necessary to scrutinize the secondary output itself.) He must watch for severe fluctuations in the frequency of reported errors, which might indicate some breakdown in the system, untrained personnel, etc. He should note any sudden cessation of reports of a particular error, which might indicate a program change and the omission of the control feature. Finally, he must be alert for obvious gaps in the errors reported, which might suggest a selective control testing only certain data, certain divisions, or certain time periods. The auditor must be aware of any controls that are not universal in application and he must understand their deviations if he is to make an accurate control evaluation. Examples of these three audit steps can be seen in Figure 40.

It has sometimes been suggested that programmed controls can be proved by means of test decks. Although test decks are useful in some situations, generally they present many difficulties. They are very difficult and time-consuming to prepare; they sometimes distort master files; the interrelationship of the runs in a large system may necessitate the testing of all runs rather than only those of interest to the auditor; they require the use of expensive computer time; true operating conditions may not prevail. If programmed controls have been evidenced by error reports during the past month, then the past month's results can be thought of as constituting one giant test deck. Why go to the trouble of running a new test deck when the results of an old one are already at hand? Of course, where, rarely, there is no historical evidence of the exercising of a given programmed control (i.e. the error in question has apparently never occurred) then a small test deck may be the only alternative. Of course, such a test deck would consist of only one or two transactions designed to test that programmed control for which historical evidence was not available. There are usually ways of running these small test decks with the client's live data to avoid the problems faced with larger test decks intended to test the complete system of control.[4]

Again, it has sometimes been suggested that programmed controls can be proved by examination of program logic and block diagrams. As has already been stated earlier in this chapter, such an examination would be an unsatisfactory method of verification for a number of reasons. It would require an extensive knowledge of programming techniques. Examining the complete program logic in order to locate a few key controls would be extremely time-consuming. There would be no easy way to establish that the block diagrams being examined represent the program actually being used to process the accounting data.

Conducting the Systems Audit

The normal analytical systems audit can be performed by tracing a few transactions (a) from their source through the input phase, (b) from last visible input to first visible output and finally, (c) through the output phase. The complete trail must be checked, including additions and calculations. (Sometimes, provided there is adequate control against the possibility of fraud, the accuracy of addition can be checked faster by a test deck designed specifically for that purpose.) Again, the systems audit can be recorded in the usual way, using file numbers and arrows. It is usually best to record the entire audit on one systems audit working paper instead of on each flow chart. Because, unlike a manual system, a complete trans-

---

[4]Whereas a full test deck is testing the accumulation and calculation of all processing information, the limited test deck is merely testing one isolated control. Therefore it is quite acceptable to have the test data rejected from further processing once the desired control has been tested. This means that there will be no distortion of master files or accounting reports. If the control to be tested will not reject the data, a subsequent control can also be intentionally violated to ensure rejection from the system.

action does not appear on one flow chart, a piecemeal systems audit recorded on each flow chart individually is difficult to follow. Recording the whole systems audit on one schedule enables the auditor to determine more easily whether or not the complete system has been tested.

In performing the systems audit, the computer processing phase normally presents no difficulty because the computer is only calculating, posting or accumulating and these operations can easily be performed manually on the data selected for the flow audit. However, when the computer is performing calculations such as invoice pricing, the systems audit must be extended to encompass all factors affecting the calculation. For instance, if the pricing varies with colour, size, quantity, customer category and sales district all these factors must be tested and proved to be influencing the pricing as purported.

Occasionally audit trail problems may develop, although this does not occur as frequently as has sometimes been suggested. When these difficulties do occur special print-outs or tape dumps can usually be arranged to bridge the gap. The details of such procedures, however, are beyond the scope of this book.

Other Effects of the Computer

The presence of a computer may have other effects on the auditor's work as well. It may affect the balance sheet audit steps he performs at the year end. It may well offer scope for audit use of the computer itself—such as in making random selection of accounts receivable for confirmation. The auditor must naturally be alert to these possibilities. The purpose of this chapter, however, has been to demonstrate solely how the pattern of the analytical audit is affected by the presence of a computer. It can be seen that while certain modifications are necessary the underlying principle of a diagrammatic analysis of systems and internal control has remained as valid for computers as for manual systems.

CHAPTER

10

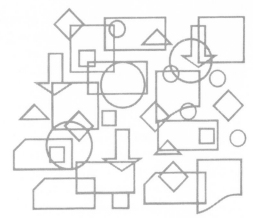

CONCLUSION

The basic design of the analytical audit was illustrated in Figure 3 and the general theory of analytical auditing was explained in Chapter 3. The succeeding chapters have reviewed in considerable detail the techniques of flow charting and the various steps comprising the systems audit and follow-up audit for both manual and automatic data processing systems. Does this description of the analytical audit approach conform to generally accepted auditing standards?

Conformity to Generally Accepted Auditing Standards

There can be little dispute about the necessity of the auditor's assessment of internal control as an integral part of the audit work. The importance of such assessment has been well accepted throughout the auditing profession for a great many years. Among the generally accepted auditing standards adopted by the American Institute of Certified Public Accountants the second standard of field work reads:

> There is to be a proper study and evaluation of the existing internal control as a basis for reliance thereon and for the determination of the resultant extent of the tests to which auditing procedures are to be restricted.[1]

The statement on *Auditing Standards and Procedures* issued by the Committee on Auditing Procedure of the same institute also states:

> Where feasible, the independent auditor's review of internal control may be conducted as a separate phase of the examination, preferably at an interim date, by applying appropriate auditing procedures directed particularly to appraising the effectiveness of the client's system. Where this is not feasible the review will usually be made in conjunction with

[1]American Institute of Certified Public Accountants, *Auditing Standards and Procedures*, 1963, p. 27.

with other phases of the audit program. A record of the independent auditor's review should be prepared in some suitable form.[2]

The approach to analytical auditing which has been outlined in this book can be seen to conform with the above statements for the following reasons:

1. A review of the system is carried out at the very beginning of the analytical audit. This review is recorded on the flow charts. Thus there is a proper study of control and it is documented.

2. A check or walk-through audit is made immediately following to prove that the charted system is really in operation—i.e. to appraise the effectiveness of the client's system. This systems audit is recorded on the flow charts as well.

3. The flow charts assist in the actual evaluation of the existing internal control by making weaknesses easy to spot.

4. Subsequent investigation is directed specifically at the weaknesses in control discovered during the systems audit. Thus there can be no question but that the review of control is defining the scope of the audit, as it should. Provision is also made for the results of weakness investigation to cause modifications in the balance sheet audit steps where appropriate.

5. The initial extents of tests in the systems audit are very restricted but this is consistent with intelligent allocation of audit effort. Strong areas are subjected to the limited systems audit tests every year together with more extended "supplementary procedural tests" on a cyclical basis every few years to confirm the auditor's judgment on control. Weak areas are subjected to a careful weakness investigation every year to establish that no material errors have occurred because of the weakness. In other words, the study and evaluation of internal control has been used to maximum advantage in determining "the resultant extent of tests to which auditing procedures are to be restricted."

Analytical auditing and the flow charting approach involve, then, no change in principles, but merely a new mechanism for serving these accepted principles in the most efficient manner.

When Analytical Auditing Can Be Used

The analytical audit approach described in the foregoing chapters can apply to all but the very small audit engagement. Where there is a formal system of office procedures and internal control an efficient audit must place reliance on the controls in force and this, in turn, implies some

[2]*Ibid.*, p. 33.

current or analytical audit to evaluate their reliability. The larger and more complex the system the more such reliance becomes essential. The very size of the system usually produces a more impregnable system of control, while the complexity of the system leads to a greater waste of audit time if the accounting reliability is ignored.

In analytical auditing the auditor is placing reliance on *structural* control: that is, the design of the system, the division of duties, the accounting controls, etc. There may, of course, be a number of weaknesses in the system but, if so, these would be investigated as a regular part of the analytical audit—as was discussed in the preceding chapters. Provided the basic framework of a control system is there, in other words, the auditor should be able to place sufficient reliance on it that he need not examine all transactions for the year. Where this is so, the analytical audit approach can provide a more thorough and, in the long run, a more efficient way of assessing the control than vouching one or two month's transactions in detail. This situation is likely to be found in all large and medium-size audits and in some small audits.

On many very small audits, however, there is little formal or structural control.[3] There would therefore be little point to a flow-chart evaluation of control which did not exist. Where the office personnel consist solely of an office manager and a bookkeeper, for instance, there might be no system of controls sufficient in itself to assure the auditor of the reliability of the accounting records. This is not to say that there would not be some controls, but they would not likely be complete enough for the auditor to place any material reliance upon them. While there might be some appropriate division of duties, the system could often be so informal that this division would not always be followed. Much might depend on the personal supervision of the office manager. Such personal control, however, does not lend itself to flow chart analysis. In these cases, the auditor's opinion on the accuracy of the accounting records must be derived not from the strength of a control system but from his knowledge of the accuracy of a large number of recorded transactions—in other words, the end-result theory. Usually, this means auditing all the transactions for a particular period; this approach may therefore be called a *period audit*. The period may vary from a month for the average small audit to several months, sometimes, for the very small audit.

---

[3]The next few paragraphs refer primarily to external audits. Organizations where internal auditors are employed will generally be of a size where analytical auditing techniques are appropriate. Therefore, the choice between 'analytical audit' and 'period audit' will usually not arise for the internal auditor.

Of course, size is not the true determining factor in choosing the audit approach. Some relatively small systems may exhibit excellent internal control while some larger systems may have extremely poor internal control. In general, it is fair to say that it would be inefficient to conduct an analytical audit where control is non-existent or where the volume of transactions is too slight to justify the set-up time required for flow chart analysis. It would be equally inefficient to conduct a period audit where control is strong and where the volume is so great that the time required to vouch all the transactions for a test period would be excessive.

Advantages of Analytical Auditing

Throughout this book analytical auditing has been described as a systems-oriented approach to auditing and most of the advantages of such an approach have been stated or implied in the course of explaining how the technique is used. It may be useful, however, to conclude with a brief summary. The advantages inherent in a systems-oriented approach are:

(a) A better understanding of the client's business and accounting system,

(b) A more comprehensive appreciation of the system of internal control,

(c) Avoidance of the risk of perfunctory and unimaginative treatment that long procedural questionnaires and audit lists may invite,

(d) Many more valuable and more realistic recommendations to clients both on internal control and on systems efficiency,

(e) Greater use of initiative on the part of audit staff in the field,

(f) A more rational allocation of audit time over those areas of the accounts requiring attention,

(g) Less chance of going through the formal motions of checking without understanding,

(h) Increased client goodwill both because of the greater productivity of audit time and because of the better briefing of new audit staff.

Of course, these advantages are not achieved without some time and effort. Clearly, a greater amount of staff training is required when this technique is employed. Moreover, there is a greater need to ensure that *all* steps in the audit program have been properly carried out. It can be seen in Figure 3 that the drawing of the flow charts themselves, while the key to the audit, is just the beginning of it. The charting can be thought of as the one-eighth of an iceberg that is visible above the surface. It is the other seven-eighths that really matters: the analysis of control once the system has been charted, the investigation of weaknesses once they have been analyzed. Without these latter steps the flow charting itself is completely useless. The charts are only a means to an end and not the end itself. Like any sophisticated technique, analytical auditing is dangerous if misused. Properly applied, however, in the hands of intelligent audit staff adequately trained, such dangers can be avoided and the many advantages realized. The technique then serves as an extremely efficient approach to the audit and a much more stimulating one for the audit staff employing it. The latter point can be of some considerable significance as the profession continues to seek increasing numbers and higher qualifications among students entering its ranks.

The flow charting approach, in short, offers both greater challenges and greater potential benefits. It is hoped that the practitioner will find, as many have already, that analytical auditing can be applied successfully in practice and that the advantages to be obtained more than repay the effort required to master the technique.

APPENDIX I

ARTICLES ON FLOW CHARTING

1. Progressive Audit Philosophy—
   The Practical Application

   The Canadian Institute of Chartered Accountants,
   Annual Conference Papers—1963 (Pg. 51-78)
   Warren Chippendale, C.A. and Norman P. LeBlanc, C.A.

2. Analytical Auditing

   The Canadian Chartered Accountant—November 1963
   R. J. Anderson, C.A.

3. Flow Charting—A Modern
   Technique in Auditing

   The Canadian Chartered Accountant—May 1964
   Vernon Turley, C.A.

4. An Approach to Auditing
   Income Accounts

   The Canadian Institute of Chartered Accountants,
   Annual Conference Papers—1964
   (Pg 186-194)
   R. J. Anderson, C.A.

5. Flow Charting—What it is and
   how you can use it effectively

   Office Equipment and Methods, March and April 1965
   George Michell

APPENDIX II

ANALYTICAL AUDIT REPORT
DESCRIPTION

SECTION I (to be completed at conclusion of systems audit)

INITIAL

I have prepared or up-dated a description of the client's business as a preliminary step to my systems review.

I have prepared or up-dated a brief organization chart of the client's personnel.

I have reviewed the systems with the employees involved, traced a few transactions over all paths of each system, and prepared or revised our flow charts to document the systems and my systems audit.

I have considered the system of internal control in the light of the flow charts, my systems audit, the lead sheet reminder questions and our previous recommendations to the client. I have described all apparent weaknesses, errors discovered and inefficiencies on our outline charts and have completed the evaluation sections on the lead sheets.

I have entered the volume statistics for the current year on the volume summary.

I have scrutinized such books of account as practical for the year to

I have reviewed the fidelity insurance, fire insurance, and other insurance carried by the client and have completed the fidelity bond and insurance coverage questionnaires. Other possible coverage for consideration might be:

I have reviewed the reports and procedures of the internal audit department (where one exists) and have taken these into account in my assessment of the internal control.

I have taken all apparent weaknesses described on the outline charts, summarized them on the weakness follow-up sheet, and drafted a proposed weakness investigation and/or revised balance sheet program to compensate for these weaknesses (taking into account any reports and procedures of the internal audit department).

I have also proposed four supplementary tests (different from last year's selection) in those areas where the control appeared adequate, to serve as a test confirmation of my assessment of the controls.

I have prepared a draft memorandum of recommendations covering the apparent weaknesses and inefficiencies summarized on the outline charts. During the audit I reported to the manager any major recommendations which should be attended to immediately. Copies of relevant memoranda from previous years are also included in the file and I have indicated thereon the disposition of each of these previous recommendations.

I have reported orally to the client any important errors I discovered and also any minor inefficiencies or system weaknesses which I thought the client might wish to attend to immediately. All significant oral suggestions have also been incorporated in my draft memorandum of recommendations.

I have completed the pertinent sections of the income and sales tax questionnaire and filed it behind my draft memorandum. Any tax recommendations arising out of this review have also been incorporated in my draft memorandum.

I have completed a time summary for the audit to date, including a suggested budget (by individual flow chart) for next year.

I have listed any uncleared notes on

The following significant changes have occurred in:

(i) the client's operations

(ii) the client's systems

In my review I noted the following inconsistencies in application of accounting principles:

In my review I noted the following items you would be interested in:

Date...   ....
                                                            Senior in charge

File reviewed
Draft memorandum of recommendations reviewed
Proposed weakness investigation approved
Proposed supplementary tests approved

Date...   ....
                                                            Manager

INITIAL

DESCRIPTION

SECTION II (to be completed at conclusion of follow-up audit)

I have further scrutinized such books of account as practical from
to

I have considered the consistency of statistical and financial data and followed up any apparent discrepancies to my own satisfaction as indicated, except:

I have carried out the weakness investigation (including additional work necessary to cover any unresolved statistical discrepancies). The results and my conclusions are outlined on   I have made a note at the front of last year's balance sheet file of any revised balance sheet steps indicated on the weakness follow-up sheet.

I have also enquired from officials of the company whether changes in personnel or systems have occurred that would affect the internal control, and where any new weaknesses were apparent have considered these in the weakness investigation.

I have carried out the four supplementary tests in those areas where the control appeared adequate. The results and my conclusions (including reconsideration of my previous control evaluation if any errors were encountered) are outlined on

I have discussed the comments and suggestions made in our draft memorandum with company employees who might be affected thereby, (using reasonable discretion), and their reaction and my resulting suggestions for modification are noted on the draft.

I have completed the time summary and the suggested budget for next year.

I have listed any uncleared notes on

I have reviewed all audit files on branch operations and have taken these into account where necessary in the weakness investigation and in the memorandum of recommendations.

During my follow-up audit I noted the following additional items you would be interested in:

Date.................. ....
                                                                    Senior in charge

Weakness investigation reviewed
Supplementary tests reviewed
Memorandum of recommendations issued and copy filed herein.

Date................. ....
                                                                    Manager

CURRENT 19   LEAD SHEET FOR SALES, RECEIVABLES, RECEIPTS   B

SYSTEMS SUMMARY

INTERNAL CONTROL EVALUATION

("Yes" answers represent apparent weaknesses) — Answer (Yes or No) — Flow chart reference

1. Can goods be shipped but not invoiced?
   Consider – (a) independent follow-up of serial continuity of *shipping or sales order numbers*?
      (b) shipping, billing segregated from cash receipts?
      (c) control of access to shipping area?
      (d) non-routine sales: scrap, fixed assets, consignment, employee sales, "direct" shipments from supplier to customer?

2. Can goods be shipped to a bad credit risk?
   Consider – (a) credit approval prior to shipment?

3. Can sales be invoiced but not recorded in the accounts?
   Consider – (a) independent follow-up of serial continuity of sales invoices?
      (b) shipping or sales order numbers tied up to documents processed *through* posting to receivables *or through* entry in sales summary?
      (c) billing segregated from receivables?
      (d) daily billing total *direct* to general ledger posting source?
      (e) daily billing total reconciled with total receivable postings?

4. Can receivables be credited improperly?
   Consider – (a) prenumbered credit note approval independent of receivables clerks?
      (b) proper support for credit notes?
      (c) independent approval of bad debt write-offs?

5. Is "lapping" possible?
   Consider – (a) receivable trial balancing, aging, review, follow-up of delinquent accounts independent of posting clerks?
      (b) checking and mailing of statements independently of posting clerks, control where no statements?
      (c) customer queries followed up independently?

6. Can payments be received and not deposited?
   Consider – (a) cashier and receivable ledger functions separated?
      (b) cheques stamped "for deposit only" when mail opened, bank accepts only for deposit?
      (c) mail receipts direct to cashier, listed, or control totals taken immediately?
      (d) deposits checked, deposited promptly?
      (e) control over branch deposit accounts?

7. Can overdue accounts escape attention?
   Consider – (a) aged trial balances?
      (b) independent follow-up?

8. Can sales be invoiced but not costed?

9. Can invoicing errors occur?
   Consider – (a) pricing, quantities, extensions checked?
      (b) standard price list, exceptions approved?

10. Can cash sales proceeds be misappropriated?
    Consider – (a) locked-in register invoice copy *or* prenumbered receipts?
       (b) independent check of prenumbered invoices to cash book?
       (c) control over drivers' collections, C.O.D. sales, etc.?

11. Can miscellaneous receipts be missed?
    Consider – (a) set up as receivable or independent check of collections?

EVALUATED BY:

INDEX OF SECTION

B1 –
B2 –
B3 –
B4 –

FLOW CHARTING GUIDE

Ensure that the flow charts cover all types of transactions involving significant differences in procedures. Consider:
1. Type of order
   – telephone, written, salesman; credit, C.O.D., cash;
2. Type of customer
   – domestic, foreign; consumer, distributor; consignment; affiliated company;
3. Type of shipment
   – shipping location, warehousing;
   – type of carrier, customer pick up, direct from supplier to customer;
   – complete, partial, backorders;
4. Type of product
   – stock, custom; product class;
5. Miscellaneous
   – fixed asset sales, scrap sales, employee sales;
Ensure that the flow charts cover all significant phases of each transaction, e.g.:
   – quoting, price determination, pricing, sales tax, outward freight, costing, returns, types of credit notes, write-offs, accounts receivable procedures, credit control, collections, discounts, etc.

156

SYSTEMS SUMMARY

INTERNAL CONTROL EVALUATION

("Yes" answers represent apparent weaknesses)

	Answer (Yes or No)	Flow chart reference

1. **Can goods be purchased if not authorized?**
   Consider – (a) purchase requisition and purchase order approvals?
   (b) purchasing segregated from receiving, accounts payable, inventory records?

2. **Can payables be set up if goods not received?**
   Consider – (a) receiving segregated from accounts payable, inventory records, purchasing?
   (b) receiving slip or other written record made?
   (c) adequate inspection, claims for short shipments, etc.?
   (d) invoices, receiving slips direct to accounts payable not purchasing?
   (e) invoices checked to purchase orders, receiving slips?
   (f) cancellation of documents and duplicates to prevent re-use?
   (g) unmatched documents investigated regularly?
   (h) freight checked, bills matched to purchases?

3. **Can payments be made if not properly supported?**
   Consider – (a) discounts taken?
   (b) control when invoices paid before validating complete?
   (c) check of extensions, additions, discounts?
   (d) two signing officers independent of purchasing, receiving, accounts payable, and cheque preparation?
   (e) first signing officer examines support for payment and approves for completeness?
   (f) second signing officer scrutinizes support?
   (g) cheques protectographed before signature, control over signature plates?
   (h) cheques mailed out directly?
   (i) payables trial balanced monthly?
   (j) independent bank reconciliation, cheques directly from bank?
   (k) reconciliations approved?
   (l) prenumbered cheques, continuity accounted for, control over unused?
   (m) bank transfers controlled?
   (n) no bearer or "cash" cheques?

4. **Can payments for non-routine purchases (e.g. of services) be made if not authorized or properly supported?**

5. **Can liabilities be incurred but not recorded?**

6. **Can charges be distributed to improper accounts?**
   Consider – (a) suppliers' statements reconciled?
   (a) distribution of purchase order, voucher distribution reviewed?

7. **Can petty cash be misappropriated?**
   Consider – (a) imprest funds, reasonable amounts?
   (b) approvals, vouchers cancelled?
   (c) periodic counts?

8. **Can fixed assets be acquired or disposed of without proper authorization and recording?**
   Consider – (a) approved work orders for fixed assets and major repairs?
   (b) approval of cost over-runs?
   (c) plant reporting of scrapping or disposals?
   (d) detailed fixed asset ledger, periodic inspection?
   (e) periodic insurance appraisals, adequate coverage?

EVALUATED BY: ....

INDEX OF SECTION

C1 –
C2 –
C3 –
C4 –

FLOW CHARTING GUIDE

Ensure that the flow charts cover all types of transactions involving significant differences in procedures. Consider:

1. Type of order
   – origin of order; miscellaneous disbursements;
2. Type of supplier
   – domestic, foreign; bought on consignment; affiliated company;
3. Type of shipment
   – receiving location;
   – air, rail, truck, pick up;
   – complete, partial;
4. Type of product
   – stock for resale, raw material, factory supply, office supply, services;
5. Miscellaneous
   – fixed assets, petty cash, funds transfers;

Ensure that the flow charts cover all significant phases of each transaction, e.g.:
– ordering, receiving, check on quantities, invoice audit, accounts payable procedures, returns, suppliers' debits, duty, sales tax, inward freight, miscellaneous disbursements, discounts, bank reconciliation, inventory control; etc.

SYSTEMS SUMMARY

INTERNAL CONTROL EVALUATION

("Yes" answers represent apparent weaknesses)

	Answer (Yes or No)	Flow chart reference

1. Can the payroll be inflated in any way?
   Consider – (a) payroll segregated from personnel?
   (b) calculations checked, division and rotation of duties?
   (c) totals reconciled independently with previous or "standard" payroll?
   (d) cheque signing segregated from preparation and distribution?
   (e) foremen and payroll segregated from pay distribution?
   (f) employee identification when distributed?
   (g) control of unclaimed pay?
   (h) *independent* reconciliation of bank account *or* test of payroll receipts for cash against payroll?
   (i) budgetary control, analysis of labour variances?

2. Can employees be paid for work not done?
   Consider – (a) clock cards used?
   (b) piece work tickets approved by foreman?
   (c) piece work counts reconciled with production records *or* counts spot checked?
   (d) control over pay for spoiled items or other "over-booking" possibilities?
   (e) salesmen's commissions checked to sales records?

3. Can other errors occur in payroll calculations?
   Consider – (a) rates and rate changes in personnel records authorized?
   (b) payroll notified in writing of additions, terminations, rate changes?
   (c) calculations checked by second employee?
   (d) payroll approvals, distribution reviewed?
   (e) imprest bank account?

EVALUATED BY: ....

INDEX OF SECTION

D1 –
D2 –
D3 –
D4 –

FLOW CHARTING GUIDE

Ensure that the flow charts cover all types of transactions involving significant differences in procedures. Consider:

1. Method of computation
   – monthly, weekly, hourly, piece work, combination; overtime, part time;
   – executive contracts for services;

2. Method of payment
   – cash, cheque, outside pay agent, bank transfer;
   – advances, pay-offs;

3. Type of employee
   – different locations, divisions, etc.;

Ensure that the flow charts cover all significant phases of each transaction, e.g.:
   – hiring, terminations, pay changes, personnel records, clock cards, work tickets, pay preparation, pay distribution, salary and labour cost distribution, deductions, approvals, etc.

LEAD SHEET FOR COST RECORDS AND INVENTORY RECORDS

E

SYSTEMS SUMMARY

INDEX OF SECTION

E1 –
E2 –
E3 –
E4 –

FLOW CHARTING GUIDE

Ensure that the flow charts and schedule of skeleton entries cover all types of cost entries involving significant differences in procedures. Consider:
1. Sales, purchases, payrolls
   – costing procedures for all transactions charted in sections B, C, and D;
2. Inventory records
   – inventory record procedures;
3. Type of cost entry
   – production entries; transfers to work in process, to finished goods, etc.
   – computation of variances, etc.
   – scrap, spoilage, cut-backs, order alteration;
   – overhead computation and allocation;
4. Cost records
   – record of actual or standard unit costs;
   – method of revision or up-dating;
   – reporting procedures;
   – communications with purchasing, sales, and accounting department.

INTERNAL CONTROL EVALUATION

("Yes" answers represent apparent weaknesses)

	Answer (Yes or No)	Flow chart reference

1. Can inventory items be lost or pilfered?
   Consider – (a) responsible storekeepers, fencing of stores where appropriate?
   (b) detailed perpetual records segregated from stock?
   (c) trial balancing of records, periodic counts?
   (d) storekeeper advises stock records *independently* re receipts from production or receiver?
   (e) requisitions used or some other control on usage?
   (f) control over items expensed but physically on hand?

2. Can inventory in production be consumed or wasted without being recorded?
   Consider – (a) control of excess material requisitions?
   (b) no hidden allowances for inventory shrinkage, etc.?
   (c) reconciliations of production counts?
   (d) scrap report required before scrap disposed of?
   (e) scrap weighed and sale proceeds checked?
   (f) reporting of obsolescence or slow movement?

3. Can work in process be charged with items and never relieved?
   Consider – (a) e.g. in at actual out at standard avoided?
   (b) all proper variances developed?

4. Is information produced by the cost system inadequate for proper control?
   Consider – (a) reliable and up-to-date standards used?
   (b) variance analysis?
   (c) overhead and other cost *allocations* reliable?
   (d) budgetary controls?

EVALUATED BY: ....

LEAD SHEET FOR BOOKS OF ACCOUNT AND GENERAL

F

SYSTEMS SUMMARY

INTERNAL CONTROL EVALUATION

("Yes" answers represent apparent weaknesses)

	Answer (Yes or No)	Flow chart reference

1. Can posting or addition errors occur in ledgers?
   Consider – (a) trial balanced monthly?
   (b) periodic reconciliation of control accounts?

2. Can incorrect journal entries be made?
   Consider – (a) adequately supported?
   (b) approved by senior accountant?

3. Is there a lack of accounting or administrative controls?
   Consider – (a) rotation of duties, regular vacations?
   (b) adequate fidelity insurance? (give details)
   (c) accounting manuals in use?
   (d) internal audit dept.?
   (e) books kept up-to-date?
   (f) budgetary controls?
   (g) adequate control over branch operations?
   (h) timely internal reports to management?

4. Do procedural changes during peak periods, slack periods, vacations, or illness result in any significant change in internal control?

5. Are there any areas where lack of competence on the part of any employee affects significantly the system of internal control?

EVALUATED BY: ....

INDEX OF SECTION

F1 –
F2 –
F3 –
F4 –

FLOW CHARTING GUIDE

Ensure that the section covers all significant accounting procedures not described in previous sections. Consider:

1. Ledger posting
   – all posting sources for sections B, C, D, and E covered;
2. Journal entries
   – general journal, recurring journal, statement entries.

Index

NOTE: *Italicized numbers refer to pages on which illustrations appear.*

Alternatives, methods of charting, 30, 44, 108, *117*
Analytical audit report, 72, 154
Analytical auditing
  advantages of, 11, 151
  applicability of, 150
  definition of, 1, 5
  objectives of, 8
  preliminary discussion of, 75
  theory of, 10
  use by internal auditors, 8
Audit trail problems, 147
Auditing in depth, 14

Balance sheet audit
  definition of, 5
  dependence on current audit, 7, 18
  effect of computer on, 147
  revisions to, 18, 64, 68
Block diagrams, 129, 140, 146
Books of account, 51, 54, 98, *102*

Charting paper, 21, 56
Check list
  for computer systems, 140
  for punched card systems, 128
Components
  of an analytical audit, 16, *17, 19*
  of an audit, 5
Computers
  as an integral part of the system, 128
  effect on balance sheet audit, 147
  effect on internal control, 138
  other effects of, 147
Correction of erroneous data, 145
Cost section
  charting of, 98, *100, 101*
  components of, 51, 97
  skeleton entries for, 98, *99*
Cost system, 97
Cradle-to-grave audit
  direction of, 43
  for computer systems, 146
  nature of, 14, 42, 53

Current audit
  definition of, 5
  effect on balance sheet audit, 7, 18
  necessity of, 6

Data processing systems, 121
Description of business, 47
Detail
  control of degree of, 54, 76
  elimination of irrelevant, 106
  elimination of unnecessary, 106, *111*, 124, *125*
Direction of audit flow, 43

EDP phase
  division of, 131, 138
  run structure analysis for, 135, *137*
  summarization of, 135, *136*
End-result theory, 10
Error frequency, 145
Error reports, 140, 143
Evaluation of internal control
  example of, 59, 87
  for computer systems, 139
  for punched card systems, 128
  method of, 17, 58
  reconsideration of, 20, 81

First-year audits, 47, 103
Flow charting
  articles on, 153
  basic design of, 21
  for audit purposes, 24
  for computer systems, 129, *130*, 131, *132, 133, 134*
  for punched card systems, 121, *123, 126, 127*
  guide, 50
  horizontal
    advantages of, 12
    concept of, 21
    symbols for, 23

Flow charting
  non-standard
    example of, 12, *13*
    problems with, 12
  of individual sections, 85
  rough flow lines for, 106, *107*
  standardized
    example of, *13*, 14
    reasons for, 12
  techniques for improving, 30, 103
Flow charts
  as a form of shorthand, 53
  clear layout in, 30, 103, *105*
  crossing lines in, 30, 106
  division of, 22, 109, *119*
  examples of, 31, *32, 40, 88, 94, 95, 101, 123, 126, 132, 133, 134*
  final, 39, 56
  modification of old, 56
  oversimplification in, 108, *115*
  purpose of, 16
  readability of, 109
  rough, 23, 53
  summary, 30, 129, *130*
  unnecessary repetition in, 106, *113*
Follow-up audit
  concept of, 18
  components of, 78
Fraud
  effect on audit, 4
  suspicions of, 65

Generally accepted auditing standards
  conformity to, 148

Hardware controls, 139

Infrequent transactions, 55
Internal auditors
  co-ordination with external auditors, 62
  extension of tests by, 16
  influence on external audit, 61, 67, 69
  use of analytical auditing by, 8
Internal control
  characteristics of, 59
  effect of computers on, 138
  evaluation of, 17, 58
  structural, 59, 150

Lead sheets, 50, 52, 58, 156
Limited tests, reasons for, 14

Manual phase (in computer systems), 131, *132, 133, 134*
Method theory, 11

Narrative
  example of, 12, *13*
  keyed to flow charts, 29
  problems with, 12

Objectives
  of an analytical audit, 8
  of an audit, 4
  of individual audit steps, 3
  of internal auditors, 8
Observation of inefficiencies, 17, 60, 72
Outline charts, 39, *41*, 56, 60, *89, 100, 127*
Output
  primary, 131, 140
  secondary, 131, 140, 143

Payrolls
  charting of, 96
  components of, 93
  example of, *95*
Period audit, 150
Peripheral controls, 139
Program logic, 128, 140, 146
Programmed controls
  nature of, 138
  necessary, 141
  proving existence of, 140, *142*, 144
  searching for, 140, 143
Purchases-payables-payments
  charting of, 93
  components of, 91
  example of, *94*

Questionnaires
  for computer systems, 141
  problems with, 50

Recommendations to client
  discussion, 81
  on efficiency, 17, 71
  on internal control, 18, 71
  on tax, 72
  oral, 72
  tests to support, 66
Reminder questions
  check list with, 128, 140
  description of, 51, 156
  purpose of, 18, 50
  use of, 52, 58
Retention of working papers, 77
Review of working papers, 16, 65, 73, 82
Run structure analysis, 135, *137*

Sales-receivables-receipts
  charting of, 87
  components of, 85
  examples of, *40, 41, 88, 89, 126, 127, 132, 133*
Scrutiny
  of document files, 43, 55
  of other records, 61
Small audits, 150
Staff training, need for, 151
Statistical discrepancies, 80

Statistics analysis, 78
Supplementary procedural tests, 16, 18, 69, 70, 81
Symbols
    explanation of, 24
    for audit purposes, 23
    for punched card systems, 122
    selection of, 23
    summary of, *46*
    template for, 23, 56
Systems audit
    basic step in, 42
    components of, 16, 44, 54, 146
    concept of, 16, 51
    numbers and letters for, 42, 69
    recording of, 39, 146
Systems changes during year, 81
Systems sections
    components of, 50
    division of working papers into, 22
    flow charting of, 85
    index of, 50
Systems summary, 50

Template, 23, 56
Test decks, 145, 146
Time summary and budget, 76

Violations of control conditions, 143
Volume summary, 57

Walk-through audit, 14
Weakness follow-up sheet, 62, *63*, 68
Weakness investigation
    concept of, 16, 18, *63*
    performance of, 80
    random selection for, 67
    relationship to weaknesses found, 14, 62, 66, 144
Weaknesses in control
    description of, 60
    recommendations on, 71
    relationship of audit to, 14, *63*
    structural, 59
    through inadequate physical control, 59
    through incompetent personnel, 59
Work assignment, 76, 83
Work scheduling, 16, 65, 75, 82